# WOMEN
## AND LAW

## UPASANA BORAH
ASSAM, INDIA and ASIA Record Holder

INDIA · SINGAPORE · MALAYSIA

# Notion Press

No.8, 3rd Cross Street,
CIT Colony, Mylapore,
Chennai, Tamil Nadu – 600004

First Published by Notion Press 2021
Copyright © Upasana Borah 2021
All Rights Reserved.

ISBN 978-1-63873-573-1

# DEDICATED TO

My Father & My Mother

Mr. Upendra Nath Borah
(Retd. Registrar Office of the Director of Secondary
Education, Assam, Kahilipara, Guwahati-19)

&

Mrs. Meghali Borah
(Retd. U.D.A Director of Town and Country Planning,
Assam, Dispur, Guwahati-6)

# CONTENTS

# PREFACE OF THE BOOK

The laws, for instance, denied ladies from holding certain positions or staying at work past 40 hours; commanded that if a man and a lady were similarly able to serve in a position, inclination ought to be given to the man; and banished wedded ladies from controlling property mutually claimed with their spouses. In reality, before 1971 the Supreme Court had never struck down as illegal any law that victimized ladies. It was not until the situation of Reed v. Reed, in that the Court pronounced that the Fourteenth Amendment restricted sex separation, similarly as it denied segregation based on race. For this situation, the Court struck down an Ohio law that gave that if a man and a lady were similarly able to be the director of an expired's bequest, the man ought to be delegated. All through the, the ACLU Women's Rights Project and different backers worked exhaustingly to set up ladies' uniformity through court difficulties and the authorization of social equality rules. They accomplished gigantic additions, striking down by far most of laws that separated among ladies and men, and revering in government and state law forbiddances against segregation. Today, barely any laws unequivocally treat people in an unexpected way. In any case, the rights that have been set up by court choice and by enactment are as yet not understood by all ladies in the United States. For the most underestimated ladies — helpless ladies, ladies of shading, migrant ladies — those rights are still a long way from a reality. Th us, the battle for ladies' privileges stays basic. This book tends to the main ladies' privileges gives today. These rights — and their infringement — emerge in numerous unique circumstances: in the work place, in schools, in lodging, in open facilities, in state or administrative guardianship, and in the conveyance of government benefits.

# OVERVIEW

In this work, Miss Upasana Borah examines the political, social, and religious factors that have determined the position of women in society. The author, recognising these issues, argues for equality, empowerment and emancipation of women, both in the public and private spheres.

The author has critically examined and discussed in the work, the following issues, among others:

1.  women's rights under the Constitution—mainly, equality, dignity, and to be free from discrimination;

2.  her right to maintenance under the personal laws of each religious group and the Criminal Procedure Code;

3.  offences against women, including, sexual harassment of women at workplace; and

4.  emerging issues defining the position of women.

The book will be of immense use to academics, students and legal practitioners in the fields of feminist jurisprudence, discrimination law, human rights law and constitutional law, labour law, and family law. It will also be of interest to social activists, NGO's etc.

# 1

# LAWS FOR THE PROTECTION OF WOMEN AT WORKPLACE IN INDIA

## ABSTRACT

Preface of the Constitution of India notice 'uniformity of status and opportunity' and have relating ensure specified by Art. 14 of the Constitution. Consequently, equivalent treatment of the two sexes is a lawful commitment and any biased activity, including yet not restricted to lewd behavior, is considered as key rights encroachment. To forestall and secure ladies against inappropriate behavior at working environment and for the powerful change of objections of inappropriate behavior, in December 2013 The Prevention of Workplace Sexual Harassment Act has been sanctioned. Critical, this law was established 15 years after the milestone instance of "Vishakha and others v. Territory of Rajasthan" and following Supreme Court's rules on the implementation of the crucial privileges of working ladies. The appeal was recorded against State of Rajasthan and Union of India after a lady, utilized as a social specialist with the Government of Rajasthan, was mercilessly assaulted for hindering kid marriage, normal practice at that timeframe. For the present, each business is obliged to give a review system to complaints if there should arise an occurrence of inappropriate behavior, thus, upholding sex balance in working environment. A working environment is characterized as "any spot visited by the representative in view of or because of the course of business, including transportation gave by the business to achieving of such excursion." This present work environment's definition covers both the coordinated and disorderly areas, along these lines, incorporates both public and private associations just as social orders, NGO or specialist co-ops, emergency clinics/nursing homes, homes or houses. This Act additionally endorses two sorts of specialists that can think about protests: the Internal Complaints Committee (ICC), which ought to be set up in an association with a lady functioning as the director, and the Local Complaints Committee (LCC), which empowers ladies in a sloppy or little foundations to move toward Government authorities to determine significant issues.

In this day and age is familiar with the term Sexual provocation. Inappropriate behavior can be distinguished as a conduct. It can overall terms be characterized as an unwanted conduct of sexual nature. Inappropriate behavior at work environment is an all inclusive issue on the planet whether it be a created country or a non-industrial country or an immature country, barbarities and brutalities against ladies is regular all over. It is an issue giving negative impact on the two people. It supposedly is going on additional with ladies sexual orientation as they are viewed as the most weak segment of the general public nowadays. Lewd behavior thusly is a major issue in the working environment and it has gotten one of those issues that get a ton of negative consideration.

KEYWORDS- Gender based divison of labour, Sexual Harassment, Labour Laws, Constitution of India.

## INTRODUCTION

Women in India from ancient times were agreed to be the most lifted up and deferential spot in the general public. During the post Vedic period they were limited to the four dividers of the house and their job stayed confined to the customary family work for cooking, support of home and raising of kids. They weren't allowed to look for any beneficial work outside the family. This ruined the monetary turn of events and decreased their social issues.[1]

Be that as it may, because of industrialization and urbanization new normal practices and qualities arose. After autonomy of the country the quantity of women to emerge from their homes for work expanded step by step. Despite the fact that entering of women into work constrained raised their financial and economic wellbeing, yet it offer ascent to numerous issues and troubles to them via misuse, separation and bleak working conditions.

A need was therefore felt, to introduce legal provisions for the protection of women at workplace. The Constitution of India itself under Articles 14, 15, 16, 23, 39, 43, 46 provide for the security of women at workplace in the country. Following the same, there has been multiple International and National Regulations for the concerned subject. The National Measures include The Factories Act, 1948, The Mines Act, 1952, The Maternity Benefit Act, 1961, The Equal Remuneration Act, 1976, The Payment of Wages Act, 1936, The Workmen's Compensation Act, 1923, Prevention of Sexual Harrassment at workplace Act, etc.

From old to in any case today, women are battling to track down her economic wellbeing and a decent spot in the general public at the time Indian women were in a need of certain laws to improve their social position and to guarantee appropriate security against mental and actual torment.[2]

---

1.   Professor Jayati Ghosh, Paper on 'What Exactly is Work? http://www.macroscan.org/cur/oct14/pdf/Exactly_Work.pdf
2.   Indira Jaising, Law Relating to Sexual Harassment at the Workplace (2014)

Around then Dr B.R. Ambedkar took certain helpful and genuinely necessary strides for Indian women. Because of the progressive changes brought by our constitution and endeavors made by Indian women, they have acquired themselves a good situation in the general public and subsequently they are dealt with similarly with men. The constitution not just awards correspondence to women, it gives the actions and answer for the issue of women' and furthermore engages the state to embrace proportions of positive methodology for women.[3]

The Constitution of India orders that women should be treated as equivalents and denies any oppression women taking all things together territories, including instruction, professional preparing, expertise advancement and business. Our Constitution additionally secures the privileges of women laborers by guaranteeing that their wellbeing and wellbeing is appropriately ensured throughout work, especially those of pregnant women.

The Constitution additionally defends the poise of women laborers and guarantees that they are given a protected work space liberated from inappropriate behavior. To satisfy the sacred order all work laws contain exceptional arrangements with respect to the wellbeing and security of women laborers by controlling their working hours and by lessening the weight women need to convey. As of late an extraordinary law has been instituted to ensure against lewd behavior at the work environment.[4]

## RESEARCH PROBLEM

It has been tracked down that the defensive estimates taken by the Government like separate latrines and washing offices,

---

3. Surinder Mediratta, Handbook of Law, Women and Employment (1st ed, 2009).
4. Alok Bhasin (2007) "Sexual Harassment Work", Eastern Book Company Publishing (P) Ltd, Lucknow.

grievance redressal committees against sexual harassment at workplace, drinking water and so on, are not either given or not satisfactorily kept up. There are essentially no clinical offices and maternity benefits. The laws, strategies and government assistance framework that are proposed for women laborers can't be viable except if they, when all is said and done, are aware of law and procure the solidarity to guarantee that laws are brought into power and the organs of general assessment and development and associations mount vigil and mediate to guarantee that the arrangements of the laws and government assistance framework are followed up on.

## FACTORS THAT INFLUENCE THE EMPLOYMENT OF WOMEN IN INDIA

There lie plethora of factors that adversely affects women's employment or their status at workplace. A broad list of such facts include:

1. *Social Factors*[5]

    a. Traditions, Tabboo and Customs

    b. Social Attitude

    c. Domestic/ Household works

    d. Early Marriages

    e. Child Care

    f. Accommodation

    g. Immobility

    h. Dependence

---

5. A.S Anand (2003) "Justice for Women", Universal Law Publishing CO. Pvt. Ltd, G.T Karnal Road Delhi.

2. *Economic Factors6*

   a.   Education

   b.   Training

   c.   Infrastructure

   d.   Payment

   e.   Unionism

   f.   Technology

   g.   Gender based divison of labour

   h.   Supplementary Income.

## LAWS RELATING TO WORKING WOMEN

Sexual Harassment at workplace broadly includes:[7]

- Physical contact and advances:

- A demand or request for sexual favours; or

- Making sexually coloured remarks; or

- Showing pornography; or

- Any other unwelcome physical, verbal or non-verbal conduct of sexual nature.

### THE PROHIBITION OF SEXUAL HARASSMENT OF WOMEN AT WORKPLACE ACT, 2013

### Process to be observed by the employers

♦   The act gives a layout about employers' prerequisites to build up a grievance instrument.

6.   Ibid.
7.   Tom Dannenbaum and Keya Jayram (2005) "Combating Sexual Harassment at Workplace", India Centre for Human Rights and Law, Mumbai.

- Section 4 sets out the foundation of an Internal Complaints Committee (ICC).

- The ICC should comprise of atleast-

  - Four individuals under the Chairperson boat of a senior lady representative,

  - Two individuals from among the representatives ideally a woman with experience in social work or legitimate information and

  - An outsider part ideally subsidiary with a non-legislative association.

- If a work environment has under 10 representatives it is hard to set up ICC. All things considered objections might be recorded at local protests council (LOC) set up at the area level.

- Section 19 expects employers' to coordinate a direction, workshops and mindfulness programs for sharpening representatives to the damages of lewd behavior and to give help to the complainant should she decide to document a police report.

Further, employers are needed to show at the work environment subtleties of the consequences incurred under penal law for indulging into the practice of such sexual harassment, the mechanism for the redress of grievance and the constitution of the ICC.[8]

## THE PROCEDURE FOR COMPLAINT

- It is the general presumption that every place employing woman employee consists of an ICC, therefore the

---

8.  Curriculum and Gender Question: The Indian Experience, Saroj Pandey ( Senior lecturer, DTEE, NCERT, New Delhi), Social Action, Vol. 46, Jan-Mar.1996.

concerned woman must file the complaint to the ICC as soon as possible.

♦ The Limitation period as prescribed under Section 9 of the Act for filing of such complaint is 3 months from the date of occurrence of such event.[9]

♦ However under exceptionally grave circumstances, this period can be further extended to the next three months. Nevertheless the burden to prove such grave or exceptional circumstance lies on the woman.

♦ The ICC further takes 90 days to conduct the enquiry starting from the date of receipt of the complaint by the woman. Meanwhile the woman may be transferred to another workplace or may be granted paid leave for 3 months upon her written request.

♦ On finish of the request, a report will be shipped off the business or the District Officer (for work environments with not many than 10 representatives) who is then obliged to make a move on the report inside 60 days.

♦ Employers are needed to guarantee ideal accommodation of reports to the District Officer.

  • Section 15 gives different elements to be thought of if pay for the oppressed woman is considered suitable by the ICC which incorporate the degree of mental injury, torment, enduring, enthusiastic misery, clinical costs caused, monetary status of the respondent, misfortune in vocation opportunity because of the episode, and the possibility of such installment in single amount or in portions.[10]

---

9.   Pandey, P.K., Sexual Harassment: A Crime Against Women (April 12, 2012).
10.  Singh, Priti, Sexual Harassment at Work Place (July 27, 2012).

- As an outcome, the charged individual faces a possibly huge monetary misfortune whenever discovered responsible by the ICC.

- The Act gives that the derivations might be produced using the respondent's compensation or wages. On the off chance that a grumbling isn't demonstrated, the ICC can educate the business or proper District Officer that no further activity is required.

## Women and The Labour Laws

### THE MATERNITY BENEFIT ACT, 1961

♦ Article 42 of the Constitution of India forces commitment upon the state to make arrangements for getting just and human states of work and for maternity help.

♦ The maternity benefit tends to provide wages of normal day by day compensation for the time of her real non-appearance quickly going before and including the day of her conveyance and for about a month and a half promptly following that day.

♦ Maternity Benefits: A woman can get maternity Benefits,[11]

- During Pregnancy

- After Pregnancy (during the early long stretches of parenthood).

- Government utilized women are entitled for maternity leave with full compensation.

- Other working women are entitled for about four months maternity benefits.

---

11. Sobha Saxena (2008) "Crimes against Women and Protective Laws", Deep and Deep Publications Pvt. Ltd, New Delhi.

- Even unmarried woman are entitled for maternity benefits.

- Only those Government representatives can profit these advantages, which have under two children.

- If a lady needs she can profit not many days before the conveyance and the excess leave after the conveyance, or she can benefit the whole leave simultaneously.

- The employer can't cause a lady to accomplish any weighty work in the last working month of pregnancy. She can decline to manage job which is genuinely tiring and included long standing hours, caring hefty burdens or any work which can jeopardize the legitimate development of kid, and so forth

♦ A lady is qualified for 45 days leave full wages if there should arise an occurrence of miscarriage.

- Complaint: Section 17-Section 17 discusses complaint that can be made to the inspector named under the Act. Section 23 discusses grumbling that might be held up in an official courtroom in the wake of debilitating the cures gave under the Act.

## Procedure to Seek Remedy

♦ The aggrieved woman may move toward the Inspector delegated under the Act.

♦ However, where she is disappointed with the orders passed by the Inspector she may move toward the Metropolitan Magistrate or a Judicial Magistrate of the equipped purview. In any case, such a case should be settled within 1 year from the date of commission of offense.

♦ Any office carrier of an enlisted Trade Union of which such a lady is a part or a Voluntary Organization enrolled under the Societies Registration Act, 1860 or any representative may likewise record a case in an official courtroom in the interest of the wronged lady.[12]

♦ The lady ought to have put 80 days of work before in a conveyance time of one year to have the option to guarantee the advantages under the Act.

♦ It is the obligation of lady guaranteeing maternity advantage to pull out recorded as a hard copy in the endorsed structure to her manager asserting her advantage and the time of leave. Such a notification might be given following conveyance moreover.

♦ Where she has neglected to give such a notification, she may apply to the Inspector who will make the vital orders of installment under the Act.

♦ Appeal against the sets of the Inspector misleads the redrafting authority which should be made inside 30 days from the date of the choice of the Inspector is imparted to her. The choice of the investigative authority is conclusive.

♦ If she is disappointed with the sets of the Inspector or the investigative power or if a bigger Question of law is included, she may move toward the court of the able ward.

♦ Where the business is liable, he is culpable with detainment at least 3 months to one year and with fine for at the very least Rs. 2000 to Rs. 5000.[13]

---

12. "Gender Justice and The Supreme Court" by Indira Jaising in Supreme but not Infallible: Essays in Honour of the Supreme Court of India B.N. 135 Kirpal, Ashok H. Desai, Gopal Subramaniam, Rajeev Dhavan and Raju Ramachandran (eds.) OUP, New Delhi 2000.

13. Dr Sahanwaz, Right To Be Born And Indian Legislative And Judicial Framework, Available At: Http://Www.Legalservicesindia.Com/Article/Article/Right-To-Be-Born-And-Indian-Legislative-And-Judicial-Framework-1833-1.Html( Last Visited On: August 17, 2015)

# THE FACTORIES ACT, 1948

## Rights of Working Women in Factories

♦ The aggrieved woman may move toward the Inspector designated under the Act.

♦ However, where she is disappointed with the orders passed by the Inspector she may move toward the Metropolitan Magistrate or a top notch Judicial Magistrate of the able ward. Notwithstanding, such a case should be recorded inside 1 year from the date of commission of offense.[14]

♦ Any office conveyor of an enrolled Trade Union of which such a lady is a part or a Voluntary Organization enlisted under the Societies Registration Act, 1860 or any investigator may likewise document a case in an official courtroom for the benefit of the wronged lady.

♦ The lady ought to have put 80 days of work before in a conveyance time of one year to have the option to guarantee the advantages under the Act.

♦ It is the obligation of lady asserting maternity advantage to pull out recorded as a hard copy in the recommended structure to her boss guaranteeing her advantage and the time of leave. Such a notification might be given following conveyance moreover.

♦ Where she has neglected to give such a notification, she may apply to the Inspector who will make the essential orders of installment under the Act.

♦ Appeal against the sets of the Inspector misleads the redrafting authority which should be made inside 30 days

---

14. Amrita dasgupta, Workplace Harassment! Know The Laws!, Available At: Http://Www.Respectwomen.Co.In/Workplace-Harassment-Know-The-Laws/ (Last Visited On: January 30, 2015).

from the date of the choice of the Inspector is conveyed to her. The choice of the redrafting authority is conclusive.

♦ If she is disappointed with the sets of the Inspector or the re-appraising power or if a bigger Question of law is included, she may move toward the court of the able ward.

♦ Where the business is liable, he is culpable with detainment at least 3 months to one year and with fine for at least Rs. 2000 to Rs. 5000.[15]

## THE EQUAL REMUNERATION ACT, 1976

♦ If two laborers are accomplishing a similar work, they ought to be paid equivalent wages.

♦ Even Article 39 of the Constitution visualizes that the state will coordinate its strategy, in addition to other things, towards getting that there is equivalent compensation for equivalent work for the two people.

♦ To offer impact to this Constitutional arrangement The Equal Remuneration Act, 1976 was passed to accommodate the installment of equivalent compensation to people laborers and for the avoidance of separation, on the grounds of sex, against women in the matter of business.

♦ People's Union for Democratic Rights v. Union of India[16]

• Duty of Employer to pay equivalent compensation to people laborers for same work or work of a comparative sort.

• No manager will pay to any specialist, at rates less ideal than those at which compensation is paid by him to the laborers of the other gender for a similar work or work of a comparative sort.

---

15. Section 94, Factories Act 1948
16. (1997) 1 SCC 301

- An business can't guarantee exclusion on the grounds of monetary lack of ability from The Equal Remuneration Act, 1976.

- No separation to be made while selecting workers.

◆ Advisory Committee:

  - The suitable government will establish at least one warning boards of trustees to exhortation.

  - Every warning board of trustees will comprise of at the very least ten people of which one-half will be women.

  - The warning advisory group will have respect to the quantity of women utilized in the concerned foundation or business, the idea of work, long stretches of work, reasonableness of women for business.

  - The warning advisory group will control its own system.

◆ Power of appropriate government to select experts for hearing and choosing cases and grievances:

  - A work official is to be selected to hear and choosing;

  - Complaints as to the contradiction of any arrangement of this Act.

  - Claims emerging out of non-installment of wages at equivalent rates to people and

  - In the instance of protest, that satisfactory strides to be taken by the business in order to guarantee that there is no contradiction of any arrangement of this Act.

  - Every authority selected will have every one of the forces of a common code under the Code of Civil Procedure, 1908 (5 of 1908), to take proof and of authorizing the participation of witnesses and convincing the creation of records.

  - An request inside 30 days yet not from that point is permitted.

- It is the obligation of managers to keep up the registers.

♦ **Powers of Inspectors:**

- To enter, at any reasonable time with such assistance as he thinks fit, any building, factory, premises or vessel;

- To require any employer to produce any register, muster-roll or other documents relating to the employment of workers, and examine such documents;

## MINIMUM WAGES ACT, 1948

♦ Every lady should be paid a similar compensation as a man for a similar sort of work i.e., equivalent to the man and not less.

♦ Women laborers should be given to the individual who work on brief premise, piece rate premise, day by day compensation, who works for a project worker or who works in agribusiness.

♦ Even assuming an individual consents to chip away at less wages, recommended by the public authority, the business will undoubtedly pay the base wages.

♦ Minimum compensation should be fixed on:

- Daily premise,

- Hourly premise and

- Monthly premise.

## PROCEDURE UNDER THE MINIMUM WAGES ACT, 1948

♦ If the business isn't paying the Minimum Wages then the work can grumbling to the work auditor.

♦ The business can't make the work for over 9 hours which incorporates the ideal opportunity for rest too.

- ♦ If the work works for over 9 hours he/she will get the additional cash which is multiplied the wages.

- ♦ Every day there ought to be one day paid rest.[17]

- ♦ Claims for installment of least paces of wages or compensation for quite a long time of rest or wages at extra time rate or according to the standards and orders made by the suitable government under this Act.

  - • The Presiding Officers of the Labor court and Deputy Labor Commissioners hear and choose claims emerging out of installment of not exactly the base paces of wages. The worker or any legitimate expert or any authority of a regd. Worker's organization or any Inspector or Any other approved individual may document a case appeal under this demonstration.

## How to document the Complaint?

- ♦ Every application under this Act should be introduced inside a half year from the date on which the base wages become payable.

- ♦ A single application might be documented in the interest of quite a few representatives.

- ♦ The Adjudicating authority will hear both the candidate and the business and after due requests may coordinate.-

  - • Payment of the contrast between the base wages to be paid under the Act and the genuine wages alongside a pay not surpassing multiple times such sum.[18]

  - • Payment of any sum because of the representatives by the business alongside pay. A Penalty of fifty rupees might be imposed on the candidate if the power feels that the application is either pernicious or vexatious.

---

17. Section 23, Minimum Wages Act 1950
18. Rule 17, Minimum Wages [Central] Rules 1950

The bearing of the authority is conclusive and he will practice every one of the forces of a common court under the Code of Civil Procedure for taking proof, implementing participation of witnesses and convincing the creation of reports. Courts have been banned from engaging suits under this Act.

- No advance will lie against the choice of the specialists under the Act.

## SOME LANDMARK CASES

1. AIR INDIA V. NARGESH MIRZA[19]

In the instant case, the Apex Court held that the regulation of Air India under which female Air hostess were to retire at the age of 33 years or if they get married within 4 years of their service or on the first pregnancy were discriminatory and violative of Article 14, 15 and 16 of the Indian Constitution. It was also held that the provision on the bar of pregnancy and the retirement is unconstitutional, it being arbitrary and unreasonable and violative of the basic fundamental rights.

2. NEERA MATHUR V. LIFE INSURANCE CORPORATION OF INDIA[20]

In the present case, LIC required female candidates to fill a questionnaire that required female candidates to provide dates about their menstrual cycle and past pregnancies. The Court held it to be invalid, since it was nothing but an invasion of privacy. The Court ordered for the restatement of the petitioner and to do away with the requirements in its future questionnaires.

---

19. AIR 1981 C 1829
20. 1992 1 SCC 286

3. VISHAKA AND OTHERS V. STATE OF RAJASTHAN AND OTHERS[21]

The Apex Court recognized that a safe working environment is a women's right. The Court also extended the definition of sexual harassment to include unwelcome sexually determined behavior, demand for sexual favours, sexually coloured remarks, showing pornography etc. It was directed that all employers have to mandatorily take strict and appropriate measures in this regard. Express prohibition had to be notified, published and circulated.

4. APPAREL EXPORT PROMOTION COUNCIL V. A.K CHOPRA [22]

The Supreme Court upheld the Vishakha Guidelines and held the dismissal of a superior officer as correct, since he was found sexually harassing a subordinate. Moreover, the Apex Court expanded the definition of sexual harassment by holding that physical contact is not essential for sexual harassment.

5. MUNICIPAL CORPORATION OF DELHI V. FEMALE WORKERS [MUSTER ROLLS] AND ANOTHER [23]

The Supreme Court recognized and upheld the right of female construction workers to be granted maternity leave by extending the scope of the Maternity benefit act to the daily wage workers. It was held by the court that both muster female workers and daily wage workers were entitled to the benefits of the act.

6. MEDHA KOTWAL LELE V. UNION OF INDIA[24]

The ruling by the Apex Court discusses the non- adherence to the Vishakha ruling guidelines. It has extensively delved into the issue and provided for the following guidelines -

21. AIR 1997 SC 3011
22. AIR 1999 SC 625
23. 2000 AIR SC 1274
24. 2012 STPL 616 SC

1. State governments are required to make the necessary amendments to the CCS Rules and standing orders within 2 months of judgment.

2. State governments must ensure the presence of requisite number of Complaints Committee in the state.

3. Sufficient mechanisms must be put in place to confirm adherence to the Vishakha Guidelines.

4. Different Councils which govern the profession must ensure that due adherence to the ruling is followed.

## WHERE LIES THE PROBLEM?

When it comes to India, about the effective execution of the laws that prevent crimes against women, it can be seen that such a large number of laws are too unable to curb the rate of such crimes. Talking about India implies we are talking about a Nation which already deals with the burden of a huge pendency of cases, corruption, a prejudiced mindset towards women, a judgmental approach in dealing with complaints by women, a marginally low conviction rate of such crimes, various safeguards in treating the accused and the like.[25]

If India has such high number of laws then the accused being afraid of them would end up murdering the victim? But this does not happen in majority of the cases. The other setback that the Nation Faces is the strict interpretation of laws even in the cases which are of heinous nature. Few such case including that of The State V. RajuThapa[26], where the accused teacher who was charged with the offence of Raping his Minor Student was acquitted on grounds of not proved 'beyond reasonable doubt' despite of the presence of clear video tapes, the Case of

---

25. Newman, For Richer, For Poorer, Till Death Do Us Part: India's Response to Dowry Deaths ILSA J. Int'l L, 109(1992).
26. (2014) Cri LJ 324.

ArunaShanbaug[27], where the victim of rape, after fighting for 13 long years with comma, succumbed to injuries without the accused being punished.

## SUMMING UP

Faithful implementation of the laws is of the essence under the rule of law for Good Governance. After all we are one of the Largest democracies which work with the objective of 'OF THE PEOPLE, FOR THE PEOPLE, BY THE PEOPLE', and women too are a subset of People! Concluding with the words present in Article 21 of the nation's Constitution,

**"No person shall be deprived of his life or personal liberty except according to procedure established by law."**[28]

---

27. (2011) 4 SCC 454.
28. INDIA CONST. 1950.

# 2

# VICTIMOLOGICAL ASPECT OF SEXUAL VIOLENCE

## ABSTRACT

The study article's aim is to examine the victimological nature of sexual harassment. Sexual harassment has also been a significant societal problem in many modern countries. Sexual violence is a multifaceted interdisciplinary topic with psychological, legal, medical, and other aspects. Sexual crime is an acute issue with a large degree of latency; the vast majority of those offences are not recorded in crime reports. Sexual abuse against women and girls, in particular, is a big concern in India and around the world. Victims of sexual assault encounter trauma, apprehension, confusion, and shifts in interpersonal relationships, despite improvements in employment and places of residence. It is worthwhile to examine the texts on stalking in order to uncover its victimological facets. In addition, the number of sexual offences against boys is increasing. Crime activity in cyberspace has also expanded in scale. Sexual abuse is a dynamic and pervasive problem that has the ability to have significant psychological, physical, and social implications. As a product of governmental labeling and identifying efforts, as well as psychiatric and research background approaches, these behaviors are now recognized to the general public as well as at the institutional stage. In reality, sexual harassment distinguishes itself through its impact on victims and their reactions: as a result of their pain, anxiety, and paranoia, certain behaviors, which are often only harassing or irritating, become offenses or illegal acts. In terms of early identification of risk conditions and assessment of key coping mechanisms, the analysis of victimological facets of persecutory actions is critical from a safety and prevention standpoint. The author aims to highlight the value of research in this area, which is still minimal, in order to find effective approaches to mitigate the negative effects of the phenomenon and to protect the victims through a research study on the subject.

KEYWORDS- Victimology, Sexual violence, Psychological, Victims, Criminals.

## INTRODUCTION

The Latin word victim historically refers to persons or animals whose bodies are to be killed to please the deity. It didn't have a sacrificial purpose to signify suffering or sorrow. In the 19th century, the idea of general accident or disability was synonymous with the word survivor. (Ladies and gentlemen, 2006)[29]. The term survivor describes someone who has suffered harm, loss or suffering as a consequence of the wrongful actions of any entity, community or association in the modern framework of criminal justice. Victimology first appeared in the forensic physicist Fredric Wertham's book on murders in 1949. The study of victims harmed by criminals was characterised. Victimology is a wissenschaftliche study of victims and victimisation in general, covering encounters with victims and offenders, investigators, courts, corrections, media and social movements, which we explain in our preface. The research of victims and victimization has the ability to reshape criminology as a whole. It may be the long-awaited conceptual change that criminology really requires, following the collapse

---

29. Spalek, B. (2006). Crime Victims: Theory, Policy, and Practice. New York: Palgrave Macmillan.

of the existing paradigms, such as the quest for sources of crime, prevention, recovery, care, and just rewards.

Jan Van Dijk, a victimology professor at Tilburg University, argued in 1999 that there are actually two main forms of victimology: general victimology and penal victimology, with significant variations arising from the concepts used to classify victims. Victimology in general is the analysis of casualties in their broadest context, including those that have been affected by events, natural disasters, conflict, and so on. The care, avoidance, and alleviation of the effects of being abused, regardless of the source, is the objective of this form of victimology. Interactionist (or penal) victimologists, on the other side, commonly view the topic from a criminological or judicial standpoint, with criminal law defining the field of research. According to Van Dijk (1999)[30], "the study agenda of this victimological stream blends concerns concerning crime causation with those concerning the victim's involvement in criminal proceedings."

While social violence behaviour is not new in the realm of human activity, its perception as an increasingly common and potentially dangerous phenomena by the general public, as well as the science community and legislators, dates back to modern times (DeFazio & Galeazzi, 2007)[31]. Described by literature and psychology in previous years, so-called nagging harassment appears today as a societal phenomenon that is being researched and tackled multidisciplinary concern, resulting in many observations and new scientific viewpoints (De Fazio & Sgarbi, 2009a)[32]. From a conceptual standpoint, social violence denotes a behavioral phenomenon, the so-called

30. Van Dijk, J.M. (1999). "Victimology introduction." Paper on the World Society of Victimology Ninth Symposium: http://rechten. uvt.nl/victimology/other/vandijk.pdf
31. DeFazio & Galeazzi, (2007). Theory, policy and practise on crime victims. Crime victims. New York: Macmillan Palgrave.
32. De Fazio & Sgarbi, (2009a). Victims and victimisation: essential reading. Essential reading. Waveland News, Illinois.

nagging harassment syndrome, as described by De Fazio and Sgarbi (2009a), in which such behaviour stems from a true disorder of relationships and interpersonal contact. However, the heterogeneity of the various practices that qualify it creates several interpretative challenges, making the creation of a single specific and all-encompassing description of the same exceedingly difficult. It is an undefined, changing phenomena that encompasses a virtually limitless variety of behaviors, some of which are by definition illegal and antisocial, while others are legal and socially acceptable expressions of ways of courtship or friendship-seeking (Luberto, 2005)[33]. The English word social aggression, which stems from the Italian language della caccia (from the verb to stalk) and basically implies to do the post to a prey, evokes in a synthetic way a behavioral trend consisting of a sequence of disruptive acts replicated over time, with observation and control characters, touch study and/or correspondence, in towards a worried or scared victim.

Regarding the phenomenon's definitive affirmation, international research (Merafina & Sgarbi, 2009) [34]unanimously recognizes the important role played by media, especially in the United States, where, in the late 1980s, there were some serious cases of harassment towards famous people, persecuted by obsessive or disturbed fans, whic Precisely in relation to these cronaca1 incidents, the media used the concept of "star-social abuse," coining an evocative word capable of polarizing popular opinion and influencing the progressive recognition of harassment as a worthy issue worthy of systemic attention as well as concrete legislative interventions. In reality, it is in this sense that California confronts the issue directly, passing the first anti-social aggression bill in 1990, which was quickly adopted by

---

33. Luberto,(2005). "Victimology: Past, Present, and Future." Criminologie 331:17–46.
34. Merafina & Sgarbi, 2009).. Sexual risk behaviours among young people in Bamenda, Cameroon. International Family Planning Perspectives. 26, 118–123.

all American states and, later, other Anglo-Saxon nations. More recently, in Europe, growing media and social coverage, as well as scientific-academic interest, have favored the implementation of new legislation aimed at criminalizing this phenomena in the last 15 years. Thus, in 2009, after a thorough and significant social and cultural discussion, our nation adopted a new class of crime under the Italian penal code, namely ISO-called "persecutory crimes," which are regulated by article 612 bicep. (Maugeri, 2012)[35]. In terms of dissemination, having acknowledged the rapid development of these behaviors, the key epidemiological data are attributable to research conducted in Anglo-Saxon countries (Hall & Smith, 2011)[36]. The main epidemiological data are attributable to research conducted in Anglo-Saxon countries first to understand the presence of nagging abuse and to systematically dedicate itself to their observation and deepening. In continental Europe, however, official statistics on the phenomenon are more constrained, with prevalence studies conducted only in a few nations, including Germany, Sweden, and Italy. Not to mention the inconsistencies that can be identified between various experiments, which are mostly due to methodological decisions (e.g., survey representativeness, concepts of social violence).

## VICTIMOLOGICAL ASPECT OF SEXUAL VIOLENCE

### PSYCHOLOGICAL ASPECT

Sexual abuse is a significant epidemic that can have long-term and damaging effects. Psychological responses to extreme sexual

---

35. Maugeri, (2012). Selected symptoms associated with sexual and physical abuse history among female patients with gastrointestinal disorders: the impact on subsequent health care visits. Psychological Medicine. 28, 417–425

36. Hall & Smith, (2011). Sexual abuse. In: The Conflict and Wellbeing World Survey. Geneva, World Health Office,. 149–181.

harassment and abuse, and the initiation of post-traumatic stress disorder. Myths and misconceptions on this topic are explored, as well as their possible impact on emotional responses and legal situations[37].

## JUDICIAL ASPECT

In the sense of sexual harassment, justice is most often associated with 'good consequences' (typically a verdict and a punitive sentence) from traditional criminal justice structures. Conventional refers to state-run criminal justice systems that are based on formal compliance protocols and structures and follow a clearly defined template, from police inquiries to convictions to conviction and retribution. Justice is a linear mechanism that involves a one-way process: the "crime" or "incident" has a clear origin which starts the search for justice in a certain sequence of processes in the criminal justice system. It's a hat, too. Justice is binary: either you do or do not; either you get a conviction or you do not get a verdict. Furthermore, in traditional justice systems and most discussions on what justice is, the individual determining justice is seldom (if ever) the victim-survivor of the hurt or violence (Holder, Robyn, 2015, 2015)[38]. It is curious that, after nearly 50 years of studies on the interactions of crime victims of criminal justice processes in common law nations, including Australia, there is an ongoing attachment to the usage of the word 'satisfaction' as a metric — that the term can obscure as much as it exposes. Though helpful for policy purposes, it teaches us nothing about the detail that people are

---

37. McGlynn, Clare, and Nicole Westmarland. (2019). "Kaleidoscopic justice: sexual violence and victim-survivors' perceptions of justice." *Social & Legal Studies* 28.2, 179-201.
38. Holder, Robyn. (2015). "Satisfied? Exploring victims' justice judgments." *Crime, Victims and Policy.* Palgrave Macmillan, London. 184-213.

asked to evaluate, is ambiguous about meaning, lacks motives and desires, and fixes identification and position[39].

## MEDICAL ASPECT

Not all victims of sexual assault have the same reaction. Any victims suffer from acute psychiatric trauma, and others suffer from short-term and/or long-term psychological issues. The level and duration of social care and/or psychiatric counseling needed by victims of abuse vary greatly based on the degree of psychological distress experienced and the victim's own coping strategies and abilities. As a result, the degree of social care for an attack is better decided on a case-by-case basis. Unfortunately, many victims of sexual harassment do not seek help; according to Campbell (36), only around 24–40 percent of victims seek help after an attack.

Both victims are female, with an average age of 24.1 years (range 5–80 years). A psychiatric evaluation was performed on the day of the attack in more than half of the incidents (52%) examined, while 84 percent happened within 72 hours of the assault. Body exams were not completed on 12 victims owing to incomplete referral (10.6 percent ). We identified one or more extra-genital fractures in 64 patients (63.4 percent), no injuries in 36 victims (35.6 percent), and inconclusive medical reports in one victim. Injuries, mostly bruises, were found on the limbs (32%), face (23%), and torso (7 percent ). Abrasions and contusions were less common, but two patients suffered lacerations. The Clinical Injury Extent Score was used to assess the assault's physical seriousness. The plurality of patients (44%)

---

39. Swart, L. A. et al. (2000). Rape surveillance through district surgeon offices in Johannesburg, 1996– 1998: findings, evaluation and prevention implications. South African Journal of Psychology. 30, 2–10.

had minor injuries, 18% had serious injuries, and one survivor had significant injuries[40].

**Table 1** Percentage of women aged 16 years and older who report having been sexual assault.

| Asia | | | | |
|---|---|---|---|---|
| China | Beijing | 1994 | 2000 | 1.6 |
| India | Bombay | 1996 | 1200 | 1.9 |
| Indonesia | Jakarta and Surabaya | 1996 | 1400 | 2.7 |
| Philippines | Manila | 1996 | 1500 | 0.3 |

# TYPES OF VICTIM OF SEXUAL VIOLENCE

Sexual harassment in a variety of contexts can take many forms. A single person or group of people may be raped (e.g., gang raps) sexually; the incident could be organised or accidental. Events are not possible. Although sexual harassment most commonly occurs in the home of the survivor (or perpetrator), it often occurs in a number of other places such as the workplace, classroom, prisons, cars, roads and open areas (e.g. parks, farmland)[41]. A sexual harassment suspect could be a date, an associate, a spouse, a family member, an intimate partner or former intimate partner, or a total stranger, but much of the time, the perpetrator is someone familiar to the survivor. There is no stereotype of a sexually abusive man; they come from all walks of life, wealthy and poor, educated and uneducated, religious and non-religious. Perpetrators may be individuals in places of power that are respected and trusted (for example, a doctor, instructor, tour guide, pastor, or police officer) and hence thus less likely to be accused of sexual assault. In periods of war

---

40.  Alempijevic, Djordje, et al. (2007). "Severity of injuries among sexual assault victims." *Journal of forensic and legal medicine*. 5, 266-269.
41.  "Medical-legal treatment guidelines for victims of sexual assault." (2003). World Health Organization.."

and military struggle, sexual harassment is widespread[42]. Abuse and sexual assault, in particular, are often used as demoralizing weapons; women are often coerced into "temporary marriages" with enemy soldiers. Women who are imprisoned can be sexually assaulted by jail guards and correctional officers[43].

## CHILDREN ABUSE

"Child sexual exploitation is described as the participation of a child in sexual conduct that he or she does not fully comprehend, is unable to provide informed consent to, or for which the child is not developmentally equipped and cannot consent, or that breaches cultural rules or social taboos." Child sexual abuse is described as sexual interaction between a child and an adult or another child who, due to age or growth, is in a position of duty, confidence, or control, with the activity intended to gratify or fulfill the other person's needs. Children's sexual abuse is a distinct phenomenon; the circumstances are often somewhat different from those of adult sexual harassment, and thus violence of this type cannot be treated in the same manner[44].

## 'RAPE AND ASSAULT AGAINST WOMEN'

Interpersonal abuse, whether sexual or nonsexual, continues to be a significant issue in many areas of the world. Sexual harassment against women has long-term psychiatric and societal consequences. Apart from sexual pleasure, sexual harassment against women is often the product of unfair power equations between men and women, both actual and imagined, and is often heavily affected by societal influences and beliefs. Gender stereotypes and representations, as well

42. Fitzgerald, Louise F. (1993). "Sexual harassment: Violence against women in the workplace." *American Psychologist*. 10, 1070.
43. Rock, P. (2002). On becoming a victim. In: Hoyle C and Young R (eds) New Visions of Crime Victims (illustrated edn). Oxford and Portland: Hart Publishing Ltd.
44. Shilling, C. Shilling, C. (2008). Bodies change: habits, crises and creativity. Thousand Oaks: WISDOM

as behaviors about sexual abuse, vary across sociocentric and egocentric societies. Feminist cultures offer women and men fair influence. Sexual abuse is more likely to arise in societies that promote male dominance and women's social and cultural inferiority. While culture is a vital element in understanding sexual harassment in its entirety, we must also consider the strengths and shortcomings of cultural institutions[45].

## SEXUAL VIOLENCE AGAINST MEN

Sexual violence against men and boys may occur in any type of confrontation, from interstate wars to civil wars to localized disputes, and in any cultural background. Both men and boys are insecure in war zones and in asylum-seeking nations. In prison, adult men and boys are equally prone to sexual harassment. Even though male victims are included in certain international tribunals' definitions of sexual abuse, many countries' domestic laws do not include male victims in their definitions of sexual violence, especially where homosexual conduct is punishable by law. The human effects of this marginalization and neglect of treatment remain uncertain. Male victims must be properly included in foreign reform efforts, as well as in national legislation prohibiting sexual harassment. Good results include the International Criminal Tribunal for the Former Yugoslavia4 prosecuting perpetrators of sexual assault against male victims and the Democratic Republic of the Congo recently expanding the offence of abuse to include male victims. Humanitarian partners must understand that sexual assault is not yet another type of torture for male victims. Sexual and gender-based violence is an especially virulent assault on personal and social identities, with psychological effects that frequently outlast those of other types of physical aggression[46].

---

45.  T. and Leach, Kearon, R. (2000). Burglary is re-examined as an attack of the 'body snatchers.' Criminology Theoretical 4(4): 451–472.
46.  Lea, J. and Young, J. (1984). What is to be Done about Law and Order? Harmondsworth: Penguin

# WORKPLACE SEXUAL VIOLENCE AGAINST WOMEN

Since women first started to operate outside the house, sexual assault has become a prevalent phenomenon in the workplace. According to large-scale polls of working people, nearly one out of every two women would be assaulted at any stage during their college or career lives. According to the evidence, harassment is degrading, frightening, and often physically violent; it usually lasts a long time; and it may have significant job-related, psychological, and health implications. This essay offers a concise overview of the prevalence and effects of sexual abuse, as well as a discussion of the social policy ramifications for science, regulation, and primary prevention. While sexual abuse of women staff and students has only recently received media and academic interest as an important topic, it has been a concern for as long as women have employed and researched outside the home. While sexual assault is now recognised as a significant obstacle to women's career advancement, it has proved challenging to research due to a lack of a widely understood concept and some consistent instrumentation that could offer comparative data through studies[47].

## MAIN EFFECTS AND CONSENQUENCES

In a victimological study of stalking, a factor of profound significance, inherent to the very essence of the practice, is defined by the effect that it creates on those who are subjected to certain activities. Persecutory actions, independent of uncertainties or definitional ambiguities, are capable of causing physical and psychological distress in the perpetrator, as well as a number of significant societal effects, owing to their persistence, poly-modality, and potential abuse. While the literature has focused mostly on the danger of physical attack by the stalker, it suggests that the more dangerous harm documented by the majority

47. Olivier, R. (1986). Human Emancipation and Scientific Realism. London: Reverse London

of victims is the result of repeated and unpleasant aggressive behavior, such as producing feelings such as terror, helplessness, and anguish. In reality, independent of the frequency of violent episodes, being exposed to frequent and continuous chases, harassment, and stalking may have a major negative effect, which is correlated with varying degrees of psychological and social harm. The emotional consequences for the victim may be serious, with a variety of typical symptoms detected by current research (Dressing, Kuehner, & Gass, 2005),[48] such as: distress, fear, increased aggression, rage, sense of guilt, shame, suspiciousness, introversion, hypersensitivity, insecurity, mistrust, sense of helplessness, anxiety, depression, nervousness, suicidal ideation, and suicidal ideation. Furthermore, a sizable proportion of victims' psychological conditions will deteriorate to the point of precipitating the emergence of medical conditions caused by the so-called Post-Traumatic Stress Disorder (PTSD). It deals with a large amount of post-traumatic effects of a significant traumatic incident (e.g., an automobile crash, a bank robbery, etc.), which appear to reoccur often after some period, such as avoidance, nightmares and recurrent reminders of stalking encounters, alertness, hypervigilance, sleep disruptions, fear, and mood deflection[49].

Beyond the possible immediate effects of the stalker's provocation or crime, persecutory actions often jeopardize the victim's physical wellbeing, as eating disorders, intensified usage of unhealthy lifestyle behaviors for compensatory reasons (eg, misuse of alcohol and nicotine, opioid use), and a number of psychosomatic symptoms of different nature are frequently recorded.

---

48. Dressing, Kuehner & Gass, (2005). The birth of the prison is discipline and punishment (2nd edn). Vintage: New York.
49. Hammers, C. (2013). Body and sexual trauma, sadomasochism. Society & Body. IOR: 1177/1357034X13477159 DOI:.

# JUDICIARY SYSTEM AGAINST SEXUAL VIOLENCE

In Chapter XVI of the Penal Law of the Republic of Latvia, liability for crimes against spiritual and sexual inviolability is contained (Criminal Offenses Against Morals and Sexual Inviolability). Whilst spiritual and sexual inviolability are inseparably linked to the concerns of the Criminal Law Chapter, the theory of criminal law conditionally divides these offences into two groups: 1) violation and inviolability of sexual equality; 2) moral breaches; (35, 2009). Abuse (Section 159); sexual assault (Section 160), sexual activity with an individual under the age of sixteen (Section 161), participation in sexual activity (Section 1621); Brothel foundation, preservation, administration, financing (Section 1631), participation in prostitution and exploitation of prostitution (Section 1631); (Section 166). This offences involve a person's sexual life – both the perpetrator and the survivor – that is, the most personal sphere of life. Very often, criminal legislation allows for criminal responsibility for a variety of offenses that are often referred to as sexual assaults. In fact, many such statutory acts are met that may be qualified under other Sections of the Criminal Code, but have as their base the subject's ability to fulfill sexual desire (3, 2003). According to L.J. Siegel, a criminologist in the US, sexual and religious offences are also categorized as crimes against public safety or the so-called crime of non-victims (15 2006), as well as sexual theft or other economic crimes. If a person gains sexual gratification by fetishism, he or she may commit robbery (20, 2000). Exhibitionist activities (Criminal Law section231; hooliganism) and official practises for sexual assault (Section 231 of the Criminal Law); necrophilia (Criminal Law section 228; corpseness); and bestiality or sodomy1 are cases of sexual crime)[50]. The most dangerous sexual crime is distinguished separately – sexual murder (intentional killing) whether it is

---

50. Kenney, J.S. (2009). Critical insights for Canadian victims of violence. Toronto: Press Inc. for Canadian Academics.

linked to violence (Section 117. article 7 of Criminal Law). In a specific order, the value of life and personal equality or sexual inviolability is included in criminal law norms, separating main and secondary rights based on an offender's experience (35, 2009)[51]. Sexual offences are sexual contacts in respect to which the participants do not knowingly agree or involve themselves without understanding the intent and consequences of the behaviour, thereby breaching the right of the victim to sexual freedom, equity and inviolability. This is a significant breach of basic rights, in particular children's rights. The term "sexual assault" refers to any real or threatened physical sexual intrusion, whether by coercion or under unjust or abusive circumstances. Censure It may include any physical strength, emotional manipulation, extortion, assault, or even situations when an entity is incapable to agree, such as alcohol, impression, sleeping or a mental inability to decide the circumstances, as well as personal involvement in prostitution and coercion. The researcher analyses the materials that are practical (justice processes, law practise), and notes that the vulnerability of the survivor and how it is violated by the criminality are relevant in many cases of sexual offence. An analysis of rulings of the Supreme Court, for example, including sections 160 and 162 of the Criminal Code, revealed that most of the girls at risk are aged 7 to 13 years. The overall death toll was 176 (144 women, 32 men and 4 children) (34, 2007)[52].

## CONCLUSION

Since illustrating some of the main principles of systemic abuse and the aspects in which this analysis can relate to victimology, it is evident that there are valid reasons for bringing the body into the analysis of victims and victimization. Social violence

---

51. Hall, M. (2010). Victims and Policy-Making: A Comparative Perspective. New York and London: Routledge.
52. Ahmed, S. (2004). The Cultural Politics of Emotion. New York and London: Routledge.

should include a theoretical and analytical basis for studying not just human subjectivity and embodiment in general, but also the particulars of geographically situated, historically connected, and communicating bodies. Much like practical realism was essential to questioning the discipline of victimology, social abuse can be interpreted as challenging the discipline to take the body's position in all forms of victimization seriously. This essay explores how the nuances of systemic violence can be extended to victimological study of the intersections of "race," "age," and "gender" of modes of marginalization and intentional victimization, as well as the effect of the criminal justice system on victimized bodies. Furthermore, I have seen how the body plays an important part in both the procurement of victim care by social workers and the actual services provided to victims of crime. The inclusion of social violence will serve as the foundation for victim and social policy while taking into consideration victims' and service providers' health and safety needs. It will also help to educate social policymakers about the suffering involved with victimization by emphasizing the cultural and social influences that influence pain perception and rehabilitation from injury. Social abuse, by shining attention on the position of feelings and the senses, has the ability to reorient victimology study agendas. Finally, structural abuse blurs the object-subject divide of victimological investigation by focusing on the researcher as a body-subject investigating abused body-subjects.

## REFERENCE

1. Spalek, B. (2006). Crime Victims: Theory, Policy, and Practice. New York: Palgrave Macmillan.

2. Van Dijk, J.M. (1999). "Victimology introduction." Paper on the World Society of Victimology Ninth Symposium: http://rechten.uvt.nl/victimology/other/vandijk.pdf

3.  DeFazio & Galeazzi, (2007). Theory, policy and practise on crime victims. Crime victims. New York: Macmillan Palgrave.

4.  De Fazio & Sgarbi, (2009a). Victims and victimisation: essential reading. Essential reading. Waveland News, Illinois.

5.  Luberto,(2005). "Victimology: Past, Present, and Future." Criminologie 331:17–46.

6.  Merafina & Sgarbi, 2009).. Sexual risk behaviours among young people in Bamenda, Cameroon. International Family Planning Perspectives. 26, 118–123.

7.  Maugeri, (2012). Selected symptoms associated with sexual and physical abuse history among female patients with gastrointestinal disorders: the impact on subsequent health care visits. Psychological Medicine. 28, 417–425

8.  Hall & Smith, (2011). Sexual abuse. In: The Conflict and Wellbeing World Survey. Geneva, World Health Office,. 149–181.

9.  McGlynn, Clare, and Nicole Westmarland. (2019). "Kaleidoscopic justice: sexual violence and victim-survivors' perceptions of justice." Social & Legal Studies 28.2, 179-201

10. Holder, Robyn. (2015). "Satisfied? Exploring victims' justice judgments." Crime, Victims and Policy. Palgrave Macmillan, London. 184-213.

11. Swart, L. A. et al. (2000). Rape surveillance through district surgeon offices in Johannesburg, 1996– 1998: findings, evaluation and prevention implications. South African Journal of Psychology. 30, 2–10.

12. Alempijevic, Djordje, et al. (2007). "Severity of injuries among sexual assault victims." Journal of forensic and legal medicine. 5, 266-269.

13. Medical-legal treatment guidelines for victims of sexual assault." (2003). World Health Organization.."

14. Fitzgerald, Louise F. (1993). "Sexual harassment: Violence against women in the workplace." *American Psychologist.* 10, 1070.

15. Rock, P. (2002). On becoming a victim. In: Hoyle C and Young R (eds) New Visions of Crime Victims (illustrated edn). Oxford and Portland: Hart Publishing Ltd.

16. Shilling, C. Shilling, C. (2008). Bodies change: habits, crises and creativity. Thousand Oaks: WISDOM

17. T. and Leach, Kearon, R. (2000). Burglary is re-examined as an attack of the 'body snatchers.' Criminology Theoretical 4(4): 451–472.

18. Lea, J. and Young, J. (1984). What is to be Done about Law and Order? Harmondsworth: Penguin

19. Olivier, R. (1986). Human Emancipation and Scientific Realism. London: Reverse London

20. Dressing, Kuehner & Gass, (2005). The birth of the prison is discipline and punishment (2nd edn). Vintage: New York.

21. ammers, C. (2013). Body and sexual trauma, sadomasochism. Society & Body. IOR: 1177/1357034X13477159 DOI:.

22. Kenney, J.S. (2009). Critical insights for Canadian victims of violence. Toronto: Press Inc. for Canadian Academics

23. Hall, M. (2010). Victims and Policy-Making: A Comparative Perspective. New York and London: Routledge.

24. Ahmed, S. (2004). The Cultural Politics of Emotion. New York and London: Routledge.

# 3

# SEXUAL HARASSMENT AT WORKPLACE

## ABSTRACT

Men and women were created in the same image to enjoy equal participation in all the opportunities equally and chances of creation yet it couldn't be carried on as ladies gradually turned into a product as it were. Lewd behavior is one of the significant social issues of all foundations as of late. Lewd behavior is available in different structures like physical, verbal, non verbal and visual lewd behavior. In an examination directed in Vellore 100 women laborers of various retail areas were considered to draw out the covered up difculties in being a working lady particularly that of sexual harassment. The research study has plainly uncovered that inappropriate behavior has been is as yet a work place issue in retails in Vellore city. The disappointment of perceiving the inappropriate behavior is a basic liberties issue that should be tended to. By tending to such issues inside the association would make balance and the laborers may appreciate work fulfillment. Inappropriate behavior is one of the significant social issues in our society. This thusly causes issues like loss of work, poise, societal position and now and then death toll. Sexual provocation is a type of sex segregation.

A new study has uncovered that very nearly 17% of women laborers in India face lewd behavior at their work place, with occurrence rates being high in both coordinated and sloppy areas (Agrawal, 2012). Further, it says that 26% of ladies, having a place with the sloppy area, are the sole providers of their families and thusly financial weakness prompts 'dread of losing the employment'. Different components are 'nonappearance of any agreeable component at the working environment', 'dread of getting demonized', and 'ignorance of existing change components'. New alumni from colleges are the most powerless focuses at the working environment. 'New ladies graduates join diverse private area organizations as students. These ladies become the obvious objectives of their nearby bosses who guarantee a compensation climb or a perpetual work' (The hours of India, Dec 30. 2012, Patna). 'Work environment tormenting' has developed significantly since the term was presented and dened as a working environment issue in Britain in the mid 1990s (Adams, 1992). In spite of this developing information and the way that cases and reports of inappropriate behavior are on the increment in India, no activity has been known to have been taken against its culprits. Inappropriate behavior at the working environment is a genuine issue that should be tended to by the public authority to guarantee a protected work space for ladies. Later data from Delhi shows that 78% of Delhi ladies were explicitly badgering in 2012 (Patnaik, 2013). Our examination study will underline the presence of this issue among a specfic gathering of retail shop women laborers which can be meant different specialists too, as it is a significant social issue.

This examination accordingly looked to uncover the pervasiveness of sexual provocation in the retails market in Vellore region and to spread out methodologies of managing the issue.

## INTRODUCTION

Since the previous decade, there has been a widespread awareness and affirmation that "Sexual Harassment" does exist and is broadly predominant at the workplace. There have been a few estimates which have been presented at the workplace by Governments, managers' and workers' affiliations everywhere on the world. Enactments, awareness campaigns, guiding and preparing of representatives have been a portion of the actions to battle and forestall "Sexual Harassment" at the workplace.

With the workforce turning out to be progressively diverse, an assortment of moral issues crop up at work. Perhaps the greatest test is sexual harassment at the work environment. "Sexual Harassment" is described by irritating sexual advances, signals, correspondences and different demonstrations focused on others. The beneficiary feels that these activities are a violation of their rights and hamper their work.

The consequences of a study led by SHRM in 2018 (Society for Human Resource Management (SHRM), 2018) drew out a genuine, surprising reality where associations have recorded an upsurge in the quantity of "Sexual Harassment" protests in the course of recent years. Both male and female workers had grumbled of sexual harassment. 37% of the associations who had participated in the study guaranteed that they had some sort of preparing given each year to representatives about "Sexual Harassment" at the workplace. 8% of the associations had plans to prepare their representatives about a similar issue in the coming year. 25% of the associations proclaimed that there had been a consistent expansion in the quantity of grumblings about "Sexual Harassment" being documented, as of late. As indicated by the ILO, "Sexual Harassment", particularly when it occurs at the work environment, turns into an obstacle in the method of giving protected and nice climate to every one of its representatives. Examination has demonstrated that the greatness of the issue of "Sexual Harassment" at the workplace has expanded as a result of incapable arrangements, absence of responsibility among administrators just as prepared labor to manage instances of workplace sexual harassment (Sharma, 2010).

In 2018, an overview led by SHRM (Society for Human Resource Management (SHRM), 2018), reports that however

94% of the respondents say that their organization has a policy set up to ensure its representatives against "Sexual Harassment", and 72% of the representatives in the US, are content with the organization's endeavors to forestall harassment, yet more than 1/3 of them accept that their workplace offers numerous circumstances and openings for harassment. The overview further draws out that consistent awareness projects can teach the group about practices are right, and which practices' should be kept away from at the workplace.

Kristin Smith, Sharyn Potter, and Jane Stapleton investigated the information introduced by the Granite State Poll in 2018 (Kristin Smith, 2019). The report shows that over half of the women and in any event 25% of the men in New Hampshire have encountered a type of "sexual Harassment" or the other at their work environment. The wide spread commonness of such episodes of Sexual harassment everywhere on the world demonstrate that, sexual harassment isn't kept to any one specific country or culture.

## SEXUAL HARASSMENT

As per the Supreme Court of India, "Sexual Harassment" alludes to "any unwanted, sexually decided physical, verbal, or non-verbal direct" (Supreme Court of India, 2013). The court has refered to specific models which range from "sexually intriguing comments about women, requests for sexual kindnesses, and sexually hostile visuals in the workplace. (High Court of India, 2013) According to Nemy (1975), the expression "Sexual Harassment "was utilized by Lin Farley at a public gathering in New York in April 1975, when she was advancing her affidavit identified with women and workplaces to the Human Rights Commission of New York.

Since the expression "Sexual Harassment" is exceptionally emotional, the Equal Employment Opportunity Commission2 of the United States of America, concocted a suitable clarification which characterized the go about as well as the idea of such activities. "Unwanted sexual advances, demands for sexual courtesies, and other verbal or actual lead of a sexual nature"(U.S. Equal Employment Opportunity Commission {EEOC}, 2009). The commission additionally proceeded to show that sexual harassment is for the most part portrayed by:

- Any demonstration or conduct which is unequivocal or verifiable and sets any terms or conditions for a person's employment.

- When an individual oddball such a demonstration or conduct, this dismissal is utilized as the defense for any work related choices which influence the individual, frequently in a negative way.

- These demonstration's or conduct bring about making an unfriendly and uncertain workplace for the individual, he/she winds up feeling threatened and unreliable, accordingly prompting an unfavorable effect on efficiency and conduct.

## SEXUAL HARASSMENT AT WORK

It was in 2013 that 'The Sexual Harassment of Women at Workplace (Prevention, Prohibition and Redressal) Act' was passed. This demonstration has given a thorough meaning of what is "Sexual Harassment". (High Court of India, 2013) Defining sexual harassment as any "unwanted, sexually decided physical, verbal, or non-verbal lead" (Supreme Court of India, 2013), the handbook delivered shows that sexually shaded comments, sexual ideas, interest for any sort of sexual courtesies, sexual photos, pictures, jokes and motions, go under the ambit of sexual harassment. In a similar demonstration, the court likewise features that causing a circumstance or climate where the lady feels compromise and uncertain at her workplace additionally establishes sexual harassment.

The demonstration has additionally characterized the idea of workplace. Workplace has been characterized as "private area association/private endeavor/undertaking/venture/foundation/foundation/society/trust/nongovernmental association/unit or specialist co-op and places visited by worker (emerging out of or over the span of employment, including transportation gave by boss to undertaking venture)" (Supreme Court of India, 2013). The workplace doesn't allude to simply any actual space or room or premises, it alludes to the conditions where such unwanted demonstrations or conduct is submitted, alludes to the climate made. In particular it extends the expression "workplace harassment" to allude to any sort of harassment during lunch times, or in any event, when heading out to and from work, over the span of work, and surprisingly outside the actual office space.

Comprehend that harassment doesn't allude to any one single demonstration or occurrence; it might allude to a progression of acts, in the equivalent or changing structures. By and large, individuals investigating the grievances of sexual harassment will in general talk about and allude to one demonstration or occasion or episode. Actually whether it is one demonstration of any of these (sexually hued comments, sexual ideas, interest for any sort of sexual kindnesses, sexual photos, pictures, jokes and motions) in segregation or in blend, the effect on the casualty is neglected (Dang, 2017).

## EFFECT OF SEXUAL HARASSMENT

"Sexual Harassment" in associations has antagonistic outcomes both for the association just as to the person in question. The outcomes can be of a quick nature just as lastingly affect both.

It prompts passionate, physical and mental disturbance in the person in question. The casualty feels disgraced, demotivated and genuinely scarred. Female casualties have regularly detailed monetary misfortunes due to being downgraded, unfit to perform well, being terminated or find employment elsewhere because of the harassment (Kristin Smith, 2019). Survivors of sexual harassment frequently fault themselves and experience a sensation of blame, experience the ill effects of rest related issues, and wind up being fretful and discouraged (Kristin Smith, 2019). Women who have been dependent upon sexual and sex harassment endure a huge misfortune in their work and enthusiastic prosperity (Emily Leskinen, 2011).

Then again, it prompts a few expenses to associations. "The expenses to associations incorporate expanded turnover and truancy, lower individual and gathering efficiency, loss of administrative chance to examine grievances, and legitimate costs, including prosecution costs and paying harms to casualties" (Welsh, 2000). An examination covering 8108 representatives of three Latin American nations in particular, Argentina, Brazil and Chile demonstrated that workers feel expanded inclination to give up positions occupations and the truancy builds (Merkin, 2008). Exploration has shown that sexual harassment is harming for the association since it brought about diminished workforce assurance, expanded non-attendance and decreased profitability (Merkin, 2008). At the point when the information on any sexual harassment occurrences spreads, it becomes "viral" quickly because of online media and innovation. Such terrible news about the association seriously harms the picture of the association particularly with regards to organizations, kindness and then some so with regards to its standing as a decent/safe work environment (Kanjamala, 2019).

## LITERATURE REVIEW

Hersch in her exploration showed that "Sexual Harassment" at the workplace has enduring consequences for the association just as the person in question, it demonstrated costlier to the casualty since they experience the ill effects of a scope of enthusiastic and actual results from such harassment. The analyst further clarifies that, "broadly acknowledged accepted procedures include the proclamation of a solid policy disallowing sexual harassment, workplace preparing, and an objections cycle that shields workers from reprisal" (Hersch, 2015).

Ali F. also, Kramar R. in their investigation of "Sexual Harassment" in Pakistani associations draw out the way that "in any event, when there are formal arrangements intended to forestall SH, social elements impact policy execution" (Ali, 2015). This means that it is important to achieve a social change in associations through preparing and other such mediations.

In an exploration led by Punam Sahgal and Aastha Dang, the nation over a poll was shipped off in excess of 750 female supervisors. From the 200 reactions they got they reasoned that the quantity of sexual harassment cases experienced by women was disturbing. Concurring the scientists support staff, staff from lower various leveled positions endure more rates of workplace sexual harassment. An inauspicious truth brought out by this overview was that when women are in lower positions or positions, they are normally reluctant and apprehensive however when they women ascend to senior levels giving them power, they become indifferent and reluctant to help or comprehend the issues of their female partners (Dang, 2017). Notwithstanding, the scientists demonstrate that numerous associations are taking proactive positions towards sexual harassments. A few associations have built up a hierarchical help to ensure women not simply by making a prompt move against the wrongdoer yet additionally offering enthusiastic help via advising to assist the casualty with beating the injury.

## CONCLUSION

The Vishaka judgment no uncertainty explained the meaning of sexual harassment, the meaning of workplace and made it compulsory for each business to have a set of accepted rules at the workplace. While giving rules to manage sexual harassment, the Court brought up the way that it was an issue of common liberties violation and accordingly associations should treat up this issue appropriately. Employment-related "Sexual Harassment" forces huge expenses on the two workers and their managers. Numerous associations have reacted by carrying out conventional approaches, complaint methods, or preparing programs. Associations should have proactive very much characterized approaches, instead of those focused on fulfilling consistence the executives prerequisites. Associations should hold preparing programs for the representatives just as hold courses and ability building programs for the individuals from the Internal Complaint Committee (ICC), which should be essential for the Anti-Sexual Harassment group. On the off chance that any policy must have an effect and powerful execution, strong preparing is an absolute necessity.

## REFERENCES

1.  Ali, F. & Kramar R. (2015). An exploratory study of sexual harassment in Pakistani organizations. Asia Pacific Journal of Management, 32(1), 229-249. https://doi.org/10.1007/s10490-014-9380-1

2.  Antecol, H. & Cobb-Clark, D. (2003). Does sexual harassment training change attitudes? A view from the federal level. Social Science Quarterly, 84(4), 826-842. https://doi.org/10.1046/j.0038-4941.2003.08404001.x

3.  Biaggio, M. K. (1990). Addressing sexual harassment: Strategies for prevention and change. M. A. Paludi (Ed.), SUNY series in the psychology of women. Ivory power: Sexual harassment on campus. New York, New York, USA: State University of New York Press.

4.  Dang, P.S. (2017). Sexual Harassment at Workplace -Experiences of Women Managers and Organisations. Economic & Political Weekly EPW, Junc 3, 2017, pp. 49-57.

5.  Emily Leskinen, L. C.-F. (2011). Gender harassment: Broadening our understanding of sex-based harassment at work. Law and Human Behavior, 35(1), 25-39. https://doi.org/10.1007/s10979-010-9241-5 PMid:20661766

6.  EY Forensic & Integrity Services. (2015, May 7). Reining in sexual harassment at the workplace; Mumbai, Maharastra, India.

7.  Gadlin, H. (1991). Careful maneuvers: Mediating sexual harassment. Negotiation Journal, 7(2), 139-153. https://doi.org/10.1111/j.1571-9979.1991.tb00610.x

8.  Haspels, N.Z. (2001). Action against Sexual Harassment at Work in Asia and the Pacific. Bangkok: ILO.

9.  Hersch, J. (2015). Sexual harassment in the workplace. IZA World of Labor, 2015: 188. doi: 10.15185/izawol.188. Retrieved from: IZA World of Labor: https://wol.iza.org/articles/sexual-harassment-in-workplace/long https://doi.org/10.15185/izawol.188

10. High court of Delhi. (2017, October 31). Retrieved from: http://lobis.nic.in: http://lobis.nic.in/ddir/dhc/VIB/judgement/01-11-2017/VIB31102017CW81492010.pdf

11. Indiankanoon.org. (2019, July 7). Retrieved from: https://indiankanoon.org. Retrieved from https://indiankanoon.org/doc/29530984/

12. Kanjamala, A. R. (2019, January 28). Constitution Of ICC Under the POSH Act. Retrieved from: mondaq.com: http://www.mondaq.com/india/x/776002/Discrimination+Disability+Sexual+Harassment/Constitution+Of+ICC+Under+the+POSH+Act

13. Kristin Smith, S. P. (2019). Half of Women in New Hampshire Have Experienced Sexual Harassment at Work. New Hampshire: The Carsey School of Public Policy at the Scholars' Repository. pp. 357.

14. Lach, D.H., Gwartney-Gibbs, P.A. (1993). Sociological perspectives on sexual harassment and workplace dispute recognition. Journal of Vocational Behavior, 42(1), 102-115. https://doi.org/10.1006/jvbe.1993.17032007

15. Lindenberg, L.A. (2003). importance of training on sexual harassment policy outcomes. Review of Public Personnel Administration, 23(3), 175-191. https://doi.org/10.1177/07 34371X0325702413214

16. Livingston, J.A. (1982). Responses to Sexual Harassment on the Job: Legal, Organizational, and Individual Actions. Journey of social issues, pp. 5-22.

17. Mackinnion, C. A. (1979). Sexual Harassment of Working Women. New Haven and London: Yale University Press.

18. McKinney, K.O. (1988). Graduate students' experiences with and responses to sexual harassment: A research note. Journal of Interpersonal Violence, 3(3), 319-325. https://doi.org/10.1177/088626084787878003003005

19. Merkin, R.S. (2008). The Impact of sexual harassment on turnover intentions, absenteeism, and job satisfaction: Findings from Argentina, Brazil and Chile. Journal of International Women's Studies, 10(2), 73-91.

20. Ministry of Women and Child Development, GOI. (2013, April 22). Retrieved from: wcd.nic.in: /wcd.nic.in/sites/default/files/Sexual-Harassment-at-Workplace-Act.pdf

21. Nachison, J.H. (1996). Sexual harassment in the workplace-how to recognise it, How to deal with it. Washinton DC: CGLAR Secretariat, World Bank.

22. Nemy, E. (1975). https://www.nytimes.com/1975/08/19/archives/. Retrieved from https://www.nytimes.com/: https://www.nytimeius.com/1975/08/19/archives/women-begin-to-speak-out-against-sexual-harassment-at-work.html

23. Orser, B. (2000). Sexual harassment is still a management issue gender diversity tool kit resource. "The Conference Board of Canada".

24. Schneider, K.T. (1997). Job-related and psychological effects of sexual harassment in the workplace: Empirical evidence from two organizations. Journal of Applied Psychology, 82(3), 401- 415. https://doi.org/10.1037/0021-9010.82.3.401 PMid:9190147

25. Sharma, P. (2010). India's first workplace sexual harassment survey reveals startling revelations. New Delhi: Centre for Transforming India.

26. Society for Human Resource Management (SHRM). (2018). Harassment-Free Workplace Series: The Executive View Topline. United Sates of America: Society for Human Resource Management (SHRM).

27. Steven V. Cates and Lynn Machin. (2012). The state of sexual harassment in America: What is the status of sexual harass-ment in the US workplace today? The Journal of Global Business Management, February 2012, 8(1), 133-138.

28. Supreme Court of India. (2013). The Handbook on "The Sexual Harassment of Women at Workplace". New Delhi: Supreme Court of India.

29. Traliant. (2018, August 14). https://www.traliant.com. Retrieved from: https://www.traliant.com/blog/ 2018/08/14/sexual-harassment-training-5-benefits-of-training-all-employees-not-just-managers/

30. U.S. Equal Employment Opportunity Commission (EEOC). (2009). Laws, Regulations and Guidance. USA: U.S. Equal Employment Opportunity Commission (EEOC).

31. Web Finance Inc. (2019, May 28). Retrieved from: Business Dictionary.com: http://www.businessdictionary.com/definition/sexual-harassment.html

32. Welsh, S. (2000, February 1). The Multidimensional Nature of Sexual Harassment: An Empirical Analysis of Women's Sexual Harassment Complaints. Toronto, Toronto, Canada. https://doi.org/10.1177/10778010022181750

# 4

# CHANGING DIMENSIONS OF RAPE LAWS

## ABSTRACT

Different types of views exist in the field of crime, rapes etc., all these explanation are spread in environments and require a complete integration to delve deeper and intense into the cause and effects of rape. There are several analyses regarding to rape laws which mainly concentrate on individual cases. We spread this literature by analyzing results more sequentially—leveraging modern cross national and longitudinal reforms information and exhibit that results of reforms have both global and national determinants, By using a latest incident of 16 December 2012 gang rape in India, this review has been analyzed and described the attitude of the victim, the protestors and the criminals who involved in this crime by using mental hypothesis. This has been also suggested for justifying rape with a view to destroy this crime from the nation. Criminal law in India administers and precludes the offenses/violations and rebuffs the individuals who perpetrate crime(s) as per the laws. All the offense/ wrongdoings carried out in India are totally considered as offenses/violations against the State. In India, for the most part criminal law includes three significant rules; Criminal Procedure code, Indian Evidence Act and the Indian Penal Code. There are other criminal laws in India like the Dowry Prevention Act, The Narcotic Drugs and Psychopathic Substances Act, and so forth. The alterations were achieved to Criminal law because of enormous change in the design of perpetrating wrongdoings.

In this advanced period, the wrongdoings have expanded definitely and the methods of commission of the violations have additionally gone through changes. The arrangements that were drafted about a century prior however stands great by and large, there are numerous offenses/violations which were never at any point thought or known about before(eg: Acid assault). With the coming of present day advancements the crooks have begun to utilize these in commission of violations (eg: following and voyeurism). The corrections have achieved changes to the at that point existing laws and have additionally instilled new sorts and types of offenses/violations and furthermore have given them new measurements and definitions.

KEYWORDS- Rape, Dimensions, India, Global

## INTRODUCTION

*"On some positions, cowardice asks the question "Is it safe?"*

*Expediency asks the question "Is it polite?"*

*And vanity comes along and asks the question "Is it popular?"*

*But conscience asks the question "Is it right?"*

*And there comes a time when one must take a position*

*That is neither safe, nor politic, nor popular,*

*But he must do it because conscience tells him it is right".*

This above quote is of Dr. Martin Luther King Jr. As per this quote which forces one to reflect on what matters most to us, solely as well as cooperatively. There are several incidents which become now common on female such as verbal abuse, sexual assault and Rape of females etc. These all crimes destroyed life of not only victim women but also challenge health of other women and spread distress between many women. This review basically analyze the issue of the rape and its origin from various cases at the macro and micro standard in India, implementing sociological, mentally and institutionally. It suggests evaluation for justifying this theory. Specifically, this study mainly investigate the root cause of rape case which happened on 16 Dec, 2012 in New Delhi which totally disturbed the nation because of its brutality.

As per the reports, near about every one out of 5 women in US, are sexually assaulted in her entire life. As per Balck et al., (2011), With time, the cases of sexually assault is an increasing and emerge as a essential cincenr in our society. Out of all sexual assault case, In 45% case, women have been sexually assaulted by their friend, collegue or companions. Most of the cases are actually not registered but sexual assault is considered as open of the most under reported crimes (Fisher et al., 2000, 2003; Rennison, 2002). In the launch of "Its On Us" campaign to end the cases of sexual assault on college campuses, As per the explanation and report of former president Barack Obama, He highlighted not only the trauma experienced by rape victims because of their assault, but also the secondary victimization several victims experience becuae of the negative reactions of those around them.

As per the explanation of Bieneck, Krahé, Gordon and Riger, (2011), dissimilar to several crimes such as robberies, murders, victims of sexual assault are especially helpless to being blamed for their violence. Nonetheless, regardless of the extensive or additional amount of investigation performed on this subject, there is little harmony of when victims blaming perhaps occur in sexual assault cases.

According to the overview of [40, 31], It create confusion that current study on victim blaming many times integrate to determining across different kinds of sexual assault. Foe e.g. as per the study of Grubb and Harrower (2008), different types of study exhibit that victim blaming among stranger and friends rape but then joined these kinds of sexual assault when discussing the impact of gendcr and supposed similarity on blame of victim.

As per the statement of Former president Barack Obama, who pointed out another essential which also neglected by everyone that shown their presence to the regular tendency to blame victims of sexual assault- the tradition, ideas and rehearsal of the character. Investigation on sexual assault and victim blame hardly concentrates on one of the 2 viewpoints such as:

a) Aspects of the observer as they affect victim blaming strength which we mainly refer to as individual factor. Many times discussed as the "rape thoughts framework"

b) Mainly concentrates on features of the victim perpetrator or properties of the assault as they impact the victim blame (Pollard. 1992). We basically refer these components as a situational components.

None of the above thoughts, monitors the third crucial factor which highly affecting the victim blame such as:

i. Social factors

ii. Institutional factors

Both these factors mainly refer to wider traditional impacts like gender roles, media and environmental sexually assault that highly contribute to an entire surroundings advertising blame of victim. The present study will also explains both situational and individual level as they affect victim blaming in collegues rape cases but will also explains the role and character of the societal level and institutional level components. Moreover, we also consider that how overall 3 types of components perhaps makes an impact on one another. Consider the below given figure for better understanding.

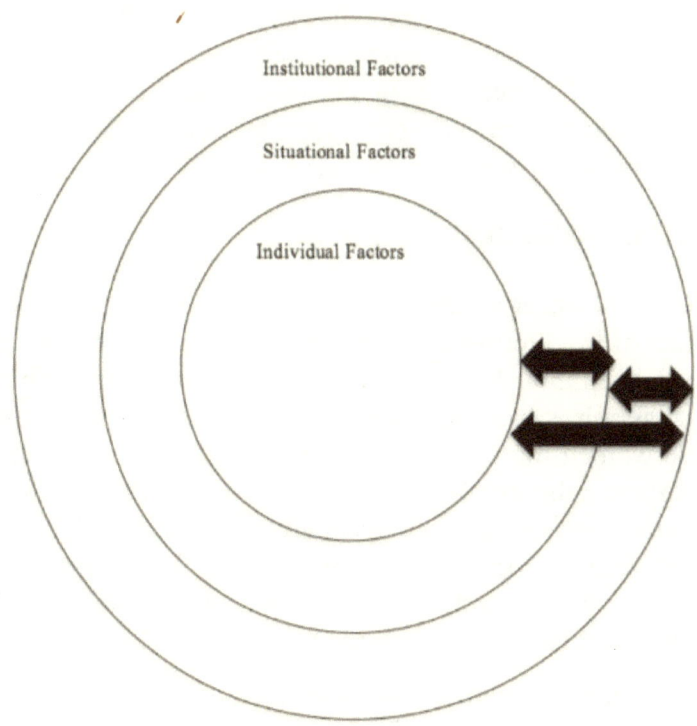

**Figure:** Conceptual model of the levels in which victim blame in sexual assault has been examined. Arrows serve to remind readers that these levels interact with one another and are not mutually exclusive.

In India, Violence based on eth gender is types of phenomenon which never ends. As per the theory of Sharma & Gupta (2013), Gender based violence makes a massive effect on the lifestyle of women, as sexual assault is intensely related to the daily life of Indian women. This type of violence can be both publicly and domestically and considered as harsh reality for women. Rape is observed as open of the appearance of gender based violence. As per [32], Now-a-days, there is mainly male-dominated society which is also one of the reasons for the gender based violence. Hence, violence is many times only recognized as a threat to body integrity and health of women. Now-a-days, Girls and women are mainly represented as "survivors" or "victims", though men are individually decreased to being a committer. This requires to be seen crucially, as men are also impacted by rape in India (Stokes, 2014).

## SEXUAL ASSAULT

As per the Hayes et al., (2013), Current origins of rape and sexual assault hardly comprised infiltration, whether it is critical, oral or anal. Even though not discounting the victimization of men, sexual assault is basically considered as the gender base crime where women more likely to be victimized in comparison to men. As per theory of [10], In fact, according to his reports, one out of every 5 women is generally assaulted in his life time. Therefore, though the male victimization is in fact challengeable, provide the highly gender nature of this crime, the present work mainly concentrates highly on the female victims.

Investigators analyze the incidence and effects of sexual assault hardly explains with 3 types of sexual assault such as:

a) Marital rape

b) Stranger rape

c) Rape by colleagues or friend

Stranger rape basically refers as a sexual assault in which there is no relationship between victim and criminal. Acquaintance rape is basically refer as when a female sexually assaulted by someone she knows very well while date rape is also refer when someone rape her during relationship (Shultx et al., 2000). At last, the assault which occurs after the marriage on female, it has been reported as a legal form of rape. The first effectively reported marital rape was reported in US in 1979 (Pagelow. 1988). These explanations perhaps not given much clear explanation as we wanted. The present review will mainly concentrate on the sexual assaults categorized as rape by colleagues and we will note separation between date rape and non-date rape where pertinent. As per the theory of the Pfeffer, (1990), date rape cases have a less chances of sentence in the court than those that fit with a stranger rape script (Larcombe, 2002).

## THE INCIDENT

The rape case on 16 dec, 2012 shocked the entire nation with brutality where a 24 year old woman was gang raped by 6 men in a moving bus. The woman was basically standing at the bus stop with her male friend and was waiting for bus to returning home at 930 pm from Saket which is generally a busy place in New Delhi. One deluxe luxury bus stopped there and they both boarded in it with assumption to as a public bus but there was only 5 passengers in the bus and all are friends of bus driver. The bus was diverted from the ordinary route and the door was locked without aware of it. After some time, the five men started tortured the woman and her friend then her friend was hit by rod and lost his conciseness then those 5 men dragged the woman inside the driver's cabin and raped in the moving bus continuously After some time, the couple was deserted out of the moving bus and then it was informed to the New Delhi Police. The police then admitted them to the hospital where it was seen that woman got serious injury by those men.

## THE AFTERMATH

Just after the incident, it was stated that the assaulters were taken into the custody within 24 hrs of the incidence. Out of 6 men, 5 were identified were in the age group 19-35 and also was in drunken state at the time of incident while the 6th assaulter was only 16 years old. The bus was also being driven illegally by the men who had no permit and allowance to pick up passengers. Just before the rape, it was also reported that these men also robbed another passengers who was carpenter.

As per the reports of hospital, the woman had suffered critical injuries because of those assaulters. The police also reported that the woman struggled bravely to fight of the assaulters but was defeated.

The woman, in extremely critical condition, was given the best possible medical care in a New Delhi hospital where her condition continued to be critical. Eventually it was decided to transfer her to an advanced multi-organ transplant speciality hospital in Singapore [12]. The woman 'fought for her' [13] life there but her condition continued to deteriorate and 'she died of cerebral edema' on 28th December 2012 [14]. Her body was flown back to India and was cremated on December 30, 2012 in Delhi under high police security. Social media played a critical role in covering the regular reporting of the situation, reaction and comments from all sections of people all over the world. This brutal incidence aklso attracted many people from the international nations. This made people angry and resulted into the mass movement of candle march on behalf of the injured woman. Several people of profession such as corporate organisations, school and college students (both boys and girls), working professionals, housewives, and common man through candle march, slogan shouting, demand for urgent action against the assaulters. The six men were charged under 'sections 307 (attempt to murder), 201 (destruction of evidence), 365 (kidnapping or abducting), 376 (2) (g) (gang rape), 377 (unnatural offences), 391 (hurting in committing robbery) and 34 (common intention) of the Indian Penal Code'. [10]

## BLAMING THE VICTIM

It basically refers to the strength to hold victims of negative occasion which is responsible for those results. As per the [9], though blaming of victim can occur in a various types of situations, which looks like specifically in case of sexually assault. It was also found that assaulters was more responsible for sexually assault her than rape.

There is currently little consensus about the predictors of victim blaming [40, 7, 21]. In fact, the sexual assault literature appears to offer only one clear conclusion: Victims of stranger rape are the least likely to be blamed for their assault; victims of marital rape are much more likely to be found culpable (Monson et al., 2000). Direct comparisons between stranger rape and acquaintance rape typically find less blame in the former case [5, 38], Further, acquaintance rape victims are blamed less than marital rape victims (Ferro et al., 2008). In short, as the victim and assailant become increasingly familiar and romantically involved, victim blame increases [9, 17, 28].

## MEASURING BLAME

Even though, the measurement of "blaming the victim" seems straight forward, still in the literature it substantially varies. The participants are generally presented by researchers in a scenario of sexual-assault case, then blame is assessed by some researchers, while perceived 'responsibility' is assessed by others, whereas blame and responsibility combined together is utilized by some and the rest assess related constructs In general, 'blame' is defined as a valuable judgment, to such an extent that one is held responsible for (and may be suffering from) a negative incident (Stormo et al., 1997) and a rating scale is usually used for typically measuring (to what extent the victim should be blamed for the assault?).'Responsibility' is defined as the extent to which the victims should be blamed for their choices or actions that significantly contributed in the assault they are blamed for. (Stormo et al., 1997), this is assessed by asking the participants to allocate a percentage of responsibility to the parties involved. Therefore, in comparison to responsibility, blame is harsher and thus the perceivers may feel more comfortable while attributing responsibility.

According to some researchers, measures of blame and responsibility can be inter-changeably used[13] while other stated these are distinguishable constructs and must be treated the same With regard to these points, the data is inconsistent. [20] found that a highly positive co-relation exists between the measures of blame and responsibility and these two measures give quite similar responses according to the intoxicated variations of the victim in case of sexual assault. Richardson and Campbell (1982) opposed, according to them the victim intoxication level does not affects victim blaming, however drunk victims are typically found more responsible for the assault in comparison to the sober victims. [34] while assessing how the victim's culpability is influenced by the dating scripts, found that men blame victims for their assault more than women, whereas no differences were found in the victim responsibility's separate measurement. Probably, the effects are non-significant on either of the measure due to floor/ceiling effects especially the ones which give higher degree of co-relation in between the constructs [21]

Ford et al., (1998) Several other related constructs such as assessment of "fault" have been used for assessing the 'victim blame' also the degree to which the victim is alleged to have "enjoyed the experience" [6, 18, 12] some professed that 'victim blaming' also happens when one fails to label a rape as a rape, even though labeling is typically used as 'manipulation check' in order to certify that the scenarios are perceived by the participants as assault [34, 28]. Several other general indicators of 'victim blame' which have not been answered with regard to a specific case comprise of - rape myth endorsement (the degree to which prejudicial, stereotyped, or false beliefs" regarding sexual assault, victims, and assailants are endorsed by the participants, pp. 217; Burt, 1980) and the Attitude they show towards the rape victims scale [38]. Nevertheless, often the results of the assessments are reflections of the beliefs they perceive on the surrounding stranger rapes (that is only in dark alleys, rapes occur) Dupuis and Clay, 2013) and for this reason it should not be considered as a measure extent of victim blame in situation such as marital or acquaintance rape. Rape myth endorsement is viewed as a potential predictor of victim blame in case of acquaintance rape, however it is not appropriate to measure victim blame.

## BEHAVIOUR OF THE CRIMINALS WITH THE HELP OF SOME PSYCHOLOGICAL THEORIES

### ERIK ERIKSON IDENTITY THEORY

Psycho-social theory of Erik Erikson gives insights specifically about the juvenile accused for a gang rape case. The model on eight stages human of development was first developed by Erikson. And in each stage a person is represented with some conflicts, that is suffering from some crises, which the person must resolve first before moving on to the very next stage, the term 'crisis' was used by [19, 28] in a sense to develop connotations of a threat, but at one point, during a crucial period vulnerability increases and potential gets heightened.

Talking of the other accused, whose detailed profiles are not found, however it is presumed due to sexual deprivation and their unknown identity in the urban surroundings (as chances of arresting unknown people are rare) can be one of the significant factor behind why they indulged in such cruel some act.

♦ **Rational Choice Theory (RCT)**

Rational Choice Theory (RCT) is the other significant theory which deals with explaining behaviour and attitude of the criminals while performing such a crime. Even though RCT genetically belongs to economics, it is also employed in various other fields [33]. This theory deals with how behaviour is effected by incentives and constraints [24]. In the field of criminology, this theory was applied by Beccaria [26], further suggested that the potential risks are purposefully weighed down by criminals against the rewards offered and then accordingly takes the decision for indulging in the crime.

Chances are there that the accused have prior accessed the risk that are involved with the activity he is planning to do out of fun and after analyzing that the punishments for such crimes are not that severe and within few days or so they may even get bail they go on to commit the crime. The main reason behind very low conviction rate of rape, is women out of social stigma hesitate to file FIR so very less number of rape cases are registered. Rape cases are dealt with leniency and often.

♦ **Social Disorganization Theory**

As SDT developed by [37], SDT means Social Disorganization Theory which basically provides another chance to investigate the case. This theory mainly argues that "crime and deviance reflect situations that destroy the integrity of local communities and decrease the strength of the regulatory power of the social norms" [6, 10]. Issue related to the marriage, migration and family problems are one of the reason to increase the probability of crime [11]

The profile of assaulter shows that 3 of them were neighbour and others were come from somewhere to New Delhi for living purpose. It also discloses that all except one were living away from their spouse for a job. The absence of family life, security and privacy led to the involvement in such crime of assaulters.

♦ **Strain Theory**

The strain theory has been developed into a social and mental theory of the crime. As per stated by [1], strain theory could be used to comprehend the way sole tackle with eh negative reactions by involving in such criminal activities. As this theory recommends that when sole are not able to attain their thoughts through approved way that they adopt various means like crime.

Most of the accused in the case belong to low social and economic standard involved in the jobs that would rarely give for their 2 square meals a day. They involved in a different types of non legal actions to satisfy their wish. They mainly used the bus for an illegal purpose; firstly they robbed a passenger of Rs 8000 who was boarded in the bus on the way. They most likely to purchase liquor from that money. After that, to satisfy the personal wish, they involved in rape crime further.

## THE GLOBAL DIMENSIONS OF RAPE-LAW REFORM

On basic exact grounds, there are valid justifications to move past home-grown factors to consider the worldwide dimensions of rape-law reform. The evidence introduced in Figure 1 strongly shows that scope extensions didn't manifest in free country contexts between 1945 and 2005, yet rather diffused in a overall wave [4]

In coming to this meaningful conclusion, we follow the lead of sociological neo-institutionalists who stress the world-social underpinnings of contemporary public activity. From the neo-institutional point of view, the truth is socially built around definitional templates that build up what exists in the world, what those existents can do, and how they interrelate (Berger and Luckmann1966; Jepperson 2002; Thomas et al. 1987). Given the drawn out expansions of present day universalism and late waves of globalization, reality's templates are progressively establishment allied in world society (i.e., incorporated into the rules of worldwide associations and the assumptions of worldwide culture).

From the neo-institutionalist domain, country states and people, specifically, are not conceived as locally situated natural actors, with inherent personalities and interests, but instead as globally-established social enactors with scripted "characters" and "interests" (Meyer etal. 1997; Meyer and Jepperson 2000). For test ple, virtually all country states instruct their citizens and stretch out testimonial to women, and they do so in exceptionally isomorphic design, according to exogenous world models (Boli and Ramirez1987; Ramirez, Soysal, and Shanahan 1997).

Virtually all country states additionally issue formal penal codes (Boyle and Meyer 1998; cf. Go2003), the incredible greater part of which has their roots in colonialization (Sanford 1988). For example, "a Criminal Code was initially introduction to the Protectorate of Northern Nigeria.|.|. Demonstrated after a code that was presented into the State of Queensland, Australia.|.|. [which]was dependent on a Criminal Code drafted in Jamaica" (Ebbe 1993). In the domain of penal codes, impersonation is plain and profoundly legitimate-ed (DiMaggio and Powell 1983; Meyer et al.1997; Strang and Meyer 1993). Nearly universal-sally, penal codes incorporate rape prohibitions.5

On these hypothetical premises, we contend that the rape-law change wave noticed between1945 and 2005 emerged from a fundamental shift in the worldwide institutional environment (Frank etal. 2008; cf. Edelman 1992; Savelsberg 1994).Stigmatized by the destructive, nationalistic, and racist overabundances of Nazism, previously dominant models of society—grounded in families, nations, and religions—offered approach to sharply individualized options in the after war era(Frank and Meyer 2002; Thomas et al. 1987).6

For instance, the world's financial and political circles reconfigured around individualized "consumers" and unsupported "electors" (mind ness the worldwide dispersion of neoliberalism and democracy). Indeed, even common issue came to be understood as persuaded by "individual actors. "The measure disembodied men and women from corporate bodies and repositioned them as autonomous people with undeniable sovereignty over their bodies and selves. Increasingly, these new models became institutionalized as natural laws and human rights[39, 27, 8].

These adjustments in the worldwide institutional environment conveyed significant ramifications for conceptions of rape. Prior to 1945, thoughts of rape retained solid corporate accentuations, prioritizing family uprightness, public honour, and male priv-ilege.7Legal limitations in this manner zeroed in tightly on extramarital vaginal intercourse, which threatened to destabilize the corporate order with "destroyed" women and "charlatan" children(Foucault 1978; Ramirez 1987).

With post bellum individualization, nonetheless, corporatist originations of rape became increasingly untenable. As people acquired always self-authority, the infringement of individual consent became an abrogating concern. Vaginal between courses consistently lost need to sexual penetration as a rule. Principles characterizing attackers as male and victims as female gave up to non-gendered originations of assailant, and laws denying the chance of rape within marriage steadily dissolved. Reconceived regarding individualized bodily integrity and independent individual decision, the scope and gravity of rape expanded and profoundened (Frank and McEneaney 1999).

In intergovernmental meetings and organizations, worldwide statements and treaties, and global affiliations and nongovernmental associations, these cycles of redefining rape occurred fundamentally inside the framework of human rights. In 1993, for instance, the United Nations General Assembly received the Declaration on the Elimination of Violence against Women, which broadcasted that "violence against women establishes an infringement of the rights and fundamental opportunities of women. "It approached states to seek after "all appropriate means and immediately [policies] eliminating violence against women."8

The moving boundaries of "rape," we argue, motivated the quick dispersion of rape-law reforms during the post bellum time. As subunits of the more extensive world social framework, country states—across social, political, and economic divides— were powerless to standardized reform templates made in world gatherings by experts and experts (counting a unit of globe-jogging law educators). These templates were scattered at such social occasions as the1995 Fourth World Conference for Women (Liu2006).9 The impacts of worldwide individualization appear in the number and considerable homogeneity of rape-law changes (i.e., their nearly universal propensity toward scope development).

The impacts likewise show up in the widespread reclassification of rape somewhere in the range of 1945 and 2005.In Poland, for instance, rape went from a Crime of Lasciviousness to an Offense against Liberty, while in Panama, rape moved from a Crime against Good Customs and the Order of the Family to a Crime against Modesty and Sexual Liberty. In the Philippines, rape transitioned from a Crime against Chastity to a Crime against Persons. These penal code renamed arrangements signal the declining centrality of the aggregate request in the theoretical contraption of rape and the climbing matchless quality of individuated people.

In certain nations, the worldwide individualization of rape likewise prodded the regrading of rape offenses during the after war time frame. Until 1989, for model, Article 315 of Paraguay's Código Penal set harsher penalties for the rape of a married lady (four to eight years in prison)than the rape of an unmarried lady (three to six years), regardless of whether the last were "a legitimate lady of good name." This differentiation rested on the grounds that the rape of an unmarried woman could be accommodated with the collective order—that is, the attacker could wed his victim. Today, such arrangements hold little authenticity and few codes actually incorporate them (Byrnes, Connors, and Bik 1997).

Rape-law amendments, regardless of how wide-spread, don't expand police detailing directly. The contextual investigation evidence demonstrates as much. Moreover, free coupling between strategies and practices is normal for worldwide organization aviation (Goodman and Jinks forthcoming; Meyer and Rowan 1977; Weick 1976). There is little motivation to expect an exception here.

## LITERATURE REVIEW

As Modi and Dada (2015, p.1) state "Female rape pulls in a ton of consideration in the sociologies, however male rape is extraordinarily ignored, in light of the fact that most scientists feature the female idea of rape." And further "No human rights instruments explicitly and comprehensively address "sexual violence against men" (pp.1-2). Subsequently, male rape portrays a genuine social and legal issue, as sexual violence against men isn't viewed as a human rights infringement and the ideas of rape are emphatically connected to a good example comprehension of women as "object of rape" and men as culprit. This is, obviously, profoundly dangerous as the lawful structure nor the socio-lawful system offers adequate help for the issue of "male rape".

The feminist discourse likewise ignored male victims previously. As [31] states "... albeit feminist clarifications of rape are strong and complete, male victims of rape have to a great extent been barred from this field of examination." The paper further looks on the building up of masculinity and the supporting of hegemonial power structures. Subsequently, the feminist discourse is yet of little assistance, both scholastically and gracefully, with regards to male rape in a socio-lawful setting. Both, enactment and feminist gatherings, have ignored the theme up until now. Despite the fact that, feminists may likewise have an interest in the nullification of "poisonous masculinity" that enables thoughts of man controlled society.

Stemple and Meyer's (2014) research has shown that there are regular fantasies and marks of disgrace encompassing male rape. For instance, that "genuine men can secure themselves" (Stemple and Meyer, 2014). This examination portrays the idea of harmful masculinity. On the off chance that a man can't shield himself from sexual violence, he isn't viewed as a "genuine man" as per this legend about masculinity. This is risky for any male overcomer of rape, as he should fear the cultural results just as "victim-accusing" and "victim-disgracing". In the event that a "male rape" survivor isn't viewed as a "genuine man" poisonous thoughts of masculinity may upset the announcing and male survivors may endure peacefully, because of the dread of taking a chance with their authentic masculinity that society requests from a "genuine man" (Stemple and Meyer, 2014).

As [30], portrays that the obstructing elements and cause behind the under reporting by male survivors. The relation with the institutional components that perhaps obstruct the reporting of male rape. If a man requires to fear from moral policing, though reporting a sexual assault or rape case, it perhaps lead to non-reporting or even a emotions of personal responsibility or blame. Identically, Masculinity has been portrayed as an issue in the fundamental context of the organization of the military where "male rape" perhaps happens but it is not much hot subject in comparison to rape of female [35].

As per the theory of Rumney's (2009), He earlier identifiers 3 barriers to the acknowledgment of male rape: denial of the issue, hierarchies of suffering and victim accusing. This also exhibit that men as rape survivors or victims perhaps capably require to fear accusing and that man who suffer from rape are as hardly hit as women or girls at the time of "rape of female".

This literature review provides a base of another overview of the present investigation. Earlier investigation portrays the ignorance of the topic and also attach to toxic beliefs of males that perhaps obstruct the reporting of "rape of male".

## CONCLUSION

Regardless of the fact that rape is basically terrible, dreadful and criminal in nature, the level and standard of the humanity of this crime has been gradually increases. This study mainly pointed out the issue of rape from various viewpoints like social, cultural, environmental and individual views and has investigate the prior Gang Rape case of New Delhi. This paper of study makes subjective and practical contribution on a less analysed topic of crime against women i.e. rape. Several advantages could accumulates from such various dimensions study of the case of rape. Comfort understanding if the encouragement behind the rape would rarely have an outcomes in taking some management to handle the issue. Moreover, legislation can be brought on less emotional bases. At last, the involvement of the victim of rape to the social and mental strain emerged by rape would be assisted.

While the assorted views found in the field of rape and associated crimes, these reviews are completely dispersed in surroundings and require a holistic combination to investigate intense into the cause and effects of rape. The current review tends to not only combine different viewpoints but also predicts a new query and line of multidimensional theories for rap as a crime against women.

## REFERENCES

1.  Agnew, R., and White, R.H. (1992), "An Empirical Test of General Strain Theory." *Criminology* 30, 475-99.

2.  Ajzen, I. (1991), The theory of planned behaviour. *Organizational Behavior and Human Decision Processes*, 50, 179-211.

3.  Allison J. A., Wrightsman L. S. (1993). *Rape: The Misunderstood Crime.* Thousand Oaks, CA: Sage Publications.

4.  Ashby, W.R., (1968), Variety, constraint, and the law of requisite variety. In: Buckley, W. (Ed.), Modern Systems Research for the Behavioral Scientist. Aldine, Chicago, IL, pp. 129-136.

5.  Ayala E. E., Kotary D., Hetz M. (2015). Blame attributions of victims and perpetrators: effects of victim gender,

perpetrator gender, and relationship. *J. Interpers. Violence* 33 94–116. 10.1177/0886260515599160 [] [] []

6.  Baron, L. and Straus, M. (1987), "Four Theories of Rape: A Macro sociological Analysis" *Social Problems*, 34, 467-489.

7.  Beneke T. (1982). *Men on Rape.* New York, NY: St. Martin's Press. []

8.  Benson B. J., Gohm C. L., Gross A. M. (2007). College women and sexual assault: the role of sex-related alcohol expectancies. *J. Fam. Violence* 22 341–351. 10.1007/ s10896-007-9085-z [] []

9.  Bieneck S., Krahé B. (2011). Blaming the victim and exonerating the perpetrator in cases of rape and robbery: is there a double standard? *J. Interpers. Violence* 26 1785–1797. 10.1177/0886260510372945 []

10. Black K. A., Gold D. J. (2008). Gender differences and socioeconomic status biases in judgments about blame in date rape scenarios. *Violence Vict.* 23 115–128. 10.1891/0886-6708.23.1.115 [] [] []

11. Blau, J.R. and Blau, P.M (1982), "The cost of inequality: metropolitan structure and violent crime." *American Sociological Review*, 47, 114-28.

12. Boparai, G.S., Nandram, S., Pula, S., Sampath, V., Sharma, R., and Singh, J. (2012), Rising incidence of rape and sex-related crimes against women in India, *Foundation for Critical Choices for India.* January. 36 p.

13. Calhoun K. S., Townsley R. M. (1991). "Attributions of responsibility for acquaintance rape," in *Acquaintance Rape: The Hidden Crime*, eds Parrot A., Bechhofer L. (New York, NY: John Wiley; ), 57–69. []

14. Calhoun L. G., Selby J. W., Warring L. J. (1976). Social perception of the victim's causal role in rape: an exploratory

examination of four factors. *Hum. Relat.* 29 517–526. 10.1177/001872677602900602 [] []

15. Duffy, K.M., Scott, L.K., Shaw, D.J, Tepper, J.B., and Aquino, K. (2012), A social context model of envy and social undermining, *Academy of Management Journal,* 55(3), 643-666.

16. Eagly A. H., Wood W. (1999). The origins of sex differences in human behavior: evolved dispositions versus social roles. *Am. Psychol.* 54 408–423. 10.1037/0003-066X.54.6.408 [] []

17. Edwards K. M., Turchik J. A., Dardis C. M., Reynolds N., Gidycz C. A. (2011). Rape myths: history, individual and institutional-level presence, and implications for change. *Sex Roles* 65 761–773. 10.1007/s11199-011-9943-2 [] []

18. Epstein J., Langenbahn S. (1994). *Criminal Justice & Community Response to Rape.* Washington, DC: DIANE Publishing. []

19. Erikson, E. H. (1968), Identity, *youth, and crisis.* New York: Norton

20. Estrich S. (1987). *Real Rape.* Cambridge, MA: Harvard University Press. []

21. Fernandes, C., Walker, R., Pricern, A., Marsden, J., and Haley, L. (1997), Root cause analysis of laboratory delays to an emergency department. *The Journal of emergency medicine,* 15(5), 735-739.

22. George W. H., Martinez L. J. (2002). Victim blaming in rape: effects of victim and perpetrator race, type of rape, and participant racism. *Psychol. Women Q.* 26 110–119. 10.1111/1471-6402.00049

23. Gerdes E., Dammann E., Heilig K. (1988). Perceptions of rape victims and assailants: effects of physical attractiveness, acquaintance, and subject gender. *Sex Roles* 19 141–153. 10.1007/BF00290151

24. Gul, S.K, (2009), "An Evaluation of the Rational Choice Theory in Criminology", *Girne*

25. Hayes-Smith R. M., Levett L. M. (2010). Student perceptions of sexual assault resources and prevalence of rape myth attitudes. *Fem. Criminol.* 5 335–354. 10.1177/1557085110387581

26. Hayward, K. (2007), 'Situational Crime Prevention and Its Discontents: Rational Choice Theory versus the "Culture of Now"', *Social Policy and Administration,* 41(3), 232–50

27. Ho C. K. (1990). An analysis of domestic violence in Asian American communities: a multicultural approach to counseling. *Women Ther.* 9 129–150. 10.1300/J015v09n01_08 [] []

28. Hofstede, G. (1980), Culture's Consequences: International Differences in Work-Related Values. Beverly Hills, CA: Sage.

29. Hofstede, G. (1998), Think Locally, Act Globally: Cultural Constraints in Personnel Management, *Management International Review*, 38(2), 7–26.

30. Javaid, A. (2015). Police responses to, and attitudes towards, male rape: Issues and concerns. International Journal of Police Science & Management, 17(2), 81-90.

31. Javaid, A. (2016). Feminism, masculinity and male rape: bringing male rape 'out of the closet'. Journal of Gender studies, 25(3), 283-293.

32. Kohn, S. (2013). Is India the Rape Capital of the World. Kole, S. K. (2007). Globalizing queer? AIDS, homophobia and the politics of sexual identity in India. Globalization

and health, 3(1), 8. Legaldrift. (n.d.). Male Rapes – Some Myths, Statistics, True Incidents and Legal Insight.

33. Lindauer, L. (2009), "Rational Choice Theory, Grounded Theory, and Their Applicability to Terrorism", *The Heinz Journal*, 9(2).

34. Maurer, T. W. & Robinson, D. W. (2008). Effects of attire, alcohol, and gender on perceptions of date rape. Sex Roles, 58, 423-434.

35. O'Brien, C., Keith, J., & Shoemaker, L. (2015). Don't tell: Military culture and male rape. Psychological services, 12(4), 357.

36. Sharma, Radha R. & Mukherjee, S. (2012) Women in India: Their Odyssey towards in In *Diversity Quotas, Diverse Perspectives: The Case of Gender*, Eds. S. Groschl and J. Takagi, Surrey: Gower Publishing, 91-115.

37. Shaw, C., & McKay, H. (1942), *Juvenile delinquency and urban areas.* Chicago: University of Chicago Press.

38. Stuart S. M., McKimmie B. M., Masser B. M. (2016). Rape perpetrators on trial: the effect of sexual assault-related schemas on attributions of blame. *J. Interpers. Violence* 34 310–336. 10.1177/0886260516640777

39. Suarez E., Gadalla T. M. (2010). Stop blaming the victim: a meta-analysis on rape myths. *J. Interpers. Violence* 25 2010–2035. 10.1177/0886260509354503

40. Turner, J. C., Hogg, M. A., Oakes, P. J., Reicher, S. D., & Wetherell, M. S. (1987), *Rediscovering the social group: A self-categorization theory.* Oxford, England: Basil Blackwellunwanted sexual experiences and distress. *J. Consult. Clin. Psychol.* 72 1090–1099. 10.1037/0022-006X.72.6.1090

# 5

# A BRIEF DISCUSSION TO WOMEN EMPOWERMENT IN INDIA: ARE WOMEN'S REALLY EMPOWERED IN INDIA?

## ABSTRACT

The Gender Ratio (alternatively the sex ratio) is one of the widely-accepted measures of the male and female constitution of the population. Woman empowerment (or the lack of it) emanates directly from this constitution. Therefore, the Gender Ratio acquires a pivotal position in any intelligent discourse involving women empowerment. A ratio of 49% to 51% would indicate a healthy trend. Globally, many countries have maintained this ratio over the decades leading to a healthy global average. However, there are some serious disparities in some countries (like India and China), where the sex ratio falls in the red zone (fewer females) (Ritchie and Roser, 2021). For every 1,000 males, India had 933 females versus 983 females globally in 2000. That is a whopping gap of 50 females per 1,000 males. Imagine the implications for a country that is the second-largest country in terms of population. The illusionary improvement in sex ratio during the preceding decade fades away given the fact that the juvenile sex ratio in 2000 had dropped from 945 females to 927 females. The problem is wide-spread across India, but some states (like Punjab, Haryana, Himachal Pradesh,

Gujrat, and Maharashtra) are particularly affected.[53] The overall drop, and particularly the drop in juvenile ratio, highlights an unfortunate prejudice against the female population even before their birth. The intrinsic female bias leads to infanticide, feticide, and ultimate economic/social exploitation. Women are denied their rights even before they are born. This is the worst kind of prejudice against a human being in any form. The disparity was perpetuated through sustained patriarchy based on social, cultural, and religious factors. Modern technology has aided and abetted female selective feticide by early identification of the sex (through ultrasound) and later through amniocentesis and abortion. Neglect, malnutrition, and unequal treatment have further led to a higher mortality rate and lower sex ratio. The outcome of such practices is "missing women" which (unnaturally) never contributed to the sex ratio. Due to the social/financial obligation of dowry, the son-preference has cemented its place in the building blocks of society. The apathy of the state (through the lack of implementation of the relevant legal framework) has aggravated the sex ratio and underlying patriarchy.

KEYWORDS- Gender Inequality, Constitution of India, Property Rights, Widow.

## INTRODUCTION

STATUS OF WOMEN: NOW AND THEN

Indian society has institutionalized gender-based discrimination through rural/urban divide, cultural values, religious injections, cast system, unfair involvement of elders, and state's failure to implement the constitutional and legal framework. Patriarchy has enjoyed sustained and deep-rooted support from male-dominated society for centuries now. Society has denied women the decision-making role even in the areas (like reproduction)

---

53. https://idoc.pub/documents/nadeem-hasnain-indian-society-and-culture-xaamin-vlr02gwkgplz

directly affecting their health and wellbeing. A woman cannot decide to have (or not) children, the number of children, abortion, feticide, or medical neglect despite the legal/constitutional cover available to her. The elders have undue influence in deciding the life partner of the girls in the family. Society expects (and outcasts) women to conform to the rules defined by the patriarchy. Their subjugated role is limited to a relationship vis-a-vis a male (like sanskari daughter to a father, an obedient wife to a husband, a hardworking mother to a son, and sadly a grieving widow to a deceased. Sometimes, the woman has to balance conflicting roles like wife and daughter-in-law. In extreme cases, it seems that the woman is married to her in-laws rather than her husband. The situation is a nightmare for women living in rural areas (India is predominantly a rural country). The caste system further compromises the cultural, social, and economic autonomy of women. Intercaste marriage is prohibited, which effectively means that a woman cannot marry the man of her choice if he belongs to another caste, religion, or sect. Religious injections, patriarchy, patriliny, and patrilocality has strengthened the caste and social system of India. The self-proclaimed superiority of the male (alternatively the inflicted inferiority on female) has led to nonconsensual confinement of women (purdah or seclusion). Men have denied the inheritance to women outrightly. Subtle and manipulative ways of securing the property (like cousin marriage) have also crept into society. Subjects like contraceptives, menstrual hygiene, and the use of condoms are taboo in society. The implicit and explicit perks of high caste have induced upward mobility in lower castes giving birth to emulation and copycats (technically known as Sanskritisation). Women, as such, become race rats against all the odds of the gap between constitutional rights and gender exploitation.

## STATUS OF WOMEN IN ANCIENT INDIA

Human race has practiced segregation and differentiation on several grounds of which the gender-based bifurcation is the primary method. Mankind has typically assigned the responsibility of bread and butter to male members, and housekeeping and reproduction to female members. Cultures based on traditionalism (like India) have ranked women inferior to men leading to patriarchy and misogyny. The role assignment has led to women being seen in perspective of their roles (as mothers, wives, sisters, aunts, and sisters-in-law) instead of their individuality as a human being. The roles come with a reverence and burden of responsibility. Each role is important as long as the woman is attached to a man. For example, a woman is socially and financially strong when she is married and becomes worthless when she becomes a widower. The sustained patriarchy has given the financial, social, emotional, and political leadership to men solely due to their gender.

## PRE-VEDIC PERIOD

Indian society remained an androcentric, patriarchal society throughout all eras, be it the Aryans, the Islamic period, the British Raj, or even modern-day India. The first documented history of India dates back to the 15th Century BC. The advent of Aryan civilization also marked the demise of matriarchy in India. One can attribute the first traces of gender-based segregation to the very beginning of the written history. Rigveda - the first known collection of Vedic hymns in Sanskrit - remained the written code of life for men and women alike. Rigveda remained valid until the 8th Century when the Islamic intrusion took segregation to a new low. The public sphere for women vanished altogether. Women remained confined to the domestic sphere while men ruled the public sphere. The British Raj of the 18th Century did not bring any relief to the exploited female segment. The patriarchy and gender segregation entangled society completely. The pre-Vedic period is obscure and shrouded in mystery, but the religious scriptures (like four Vedas including their subdivisions, Maha Puranas and Upa Puranas, Upanishads dealing with spirituality, and Epics) are replete with the bravery and tireless battles of feminism against equally relentless patriarchy.

## WOMEN IN VEDIC LITERATURE

The Vedic period marks the transition of humans from nomads to dwellers. The dwelling brought respect and companionship for women where the men were supposedly incomplete without the company of a refined woman. Even the Gods would accept the forfeit and material from married men only. The residency concept made the women needed, respected and independent in their domestic sphere. They were entrusted with the upbringing of the next generation. The new role exalted the status of women in the eyes of society. The male counterparts respected females in their roles as mothers, daughters, wives, and daughters-in-law. Even the widows enjoyed reverence from their family. The unfortunate tradition of Sati was non-existent.

## WOMEN DURING LATER VEDIC AGE

The epic Hindu literature (comprising of Ramayana, Mahabharata, and Bhagavad Gita) offers a picturesque account of male-female interaction in the post-Vedic era. The literature provides valuable insight into society and its fabric, particularly the institution of marriage. It provides the guiding principles for the generations to follow. A notable mention from that era is Svayamvara which literally means self groom. The adolescent girl went through an elaborate process of selecting her life partner which offered her the freedom to choose from a group of suitors. The bride would garland her future husband who would feel honoured by the selection. Ramayana quotes Sita and Mahabharata quotes Draupati married under the ritual of Svayamvara. One cannot term the selection as freedom in the strict sense because it was, after all, primitive and crude. The group of suitors was restricted to mighty opponents. The ritual manifested the military might of the prospective husband more than the freedom of choice for the bride. Nevertheless, the ritual relayed the final choice to the bride rather than a self-proclaimed protector of the bride. One of the notable mentions is Arjuna in the Gita. Arjuna is a staunch supporter of family values and an opponent of corruption and lawlessness among women. One of the female characters is Gandhari who showed empathy and conformity to her blind husband by blind-folding herself for the rest of her life.

## STATUS OF WOMEN IN MEDIEVAL INDIA: VERIFIABLE REFERENCES TO WOMEN IN EARLY MEDIEVAL PERIOD

The legacy of subjugation and inferiority of women continued from the post-Vedic era to medieval times. Women were creatures of a lesser god with lower intellectual and social status. They did not even deserve to understand or ponder over the religious scriptures. Society dealt a mighty blow to the right of education by lowering the eligibility age. The extreme measures from the patriarchy, however, could not contain the female populace from expressing itself. Women became an integral part of the courts and harems of influential men of society. They developed themselves in fine arts like Sanskrit and Prakrit refrains, painting, music, dance, verse, and other intellectual forms of expressive arts. Society demanded across-the-board conformity from its female members. Patriarchy spared nobody regardless of her social status (from the princess and elite class to mistress and prostitute). The written religious scriptures (Smriti) lowered the age limits for puberty and marriage. A girl had to break her association with the family at the tender age of 6 to 8 years. Society accorded heredity and property rights to the women but never refrained from compromising the freedom which comes with this right. To safeguard the family property, the female could acquire the property of her male relations. Even the widow could keep bequest if the family did not have male heirs to the deceased. After the widow, even the underage girls and the female heirs could keep the property. The medieval time, as such, marks the introduction of private property to society. Even the notorious ritual of Sati remained controversial for Smriti and external journalists (renowned Arab authors like Sulaiman). The concept of Purdah was totally optional (and a rare phenomenon). The span of medieval time was 500 years before the start of the Islamic rule (the Delhi Sultanate and the Mughal emperors). This era introduced a new breed of the female which epitomised prowess coupled with the delicate sense of fine arts. One can quote countless examples from that historic era. To start with, Razia Sultana was the first lady to grace the throne of Delhi and successfully so. That era produced legendary stateswomen like Nur Jahan and Jahan Ara who were the epitome of grandeur, military expertise, and fine taste for performing arts. Mumtaj Mahal was the first prominent female scholar in the erstwhile androcentric society. The notable mentions from the royal families are Jehan Ara, Roshan Ara, and Zaib-un-Nisa, who not only ruled the courts but also contributed to the literary collection of the time. Other noticeable mentions are Chand Bibi (the male-garbed defender of Ahmed Nager), Tara Bai (the opponent fighter against Aurangzeb), Rani Mangammal (the fierce queen of Madurai Nayak kingdom), Ahalya Bai Holkar (the most effective woman in a managerial role).

The mayhem and chaos resulting from continuous battles introduced many social vices to Indian society. Female infanticide, alive cremation of the widow with the husband, underage marriages, polygamy, and female confinement (like Purdah and Zenana versus Mardana) were rampant in the society. The menace of polygamy affected the Hindu and the Muslim population alike. A Muslim male could marry four females according to his religious injections. The Hindu male could marry even more than four women of his choice. Islam assigned the leadership to the male members leaving the female family members to unconditional obedience and subjugation. The authority of the male was unquestionable and incontestable. The Rajput segment witnessed the female infanticide due to the belief that Samskaras could only be performed by an innocent soul for salvation to be achieved.

Elements Led To The Enhancement Of Status Of Women In Modern

# SOCIETY

The improvement in the situation with ladies in the general public can be broke down in the light of the major changes that have occurred in zones like enactments, schooling, monetary and work area, political cooperation and familiarity with their privileges with respect to women, and so forth Following are a few changes:

## WOMEN IN THE FIELD OF INSTRUCTION OF EDUCATION

The impacts of women schooling on advancement establish a critical zone of exploration inside worldwide turn of events. An expansion in the measure of women's training in locales will in general correspond with undeniable degrees of improvement. A portion of the impacts are identified with monetary turn of events. Teaching young women prompts various social advantages, including many identified with women strengthening. Later research in human advancement has set up a solid connection between women schooling and global development. In specific, specialists look to figure out what components clarify contrasts in paces of advancement. Women schooling is one of the major illustrative factors behind the paces of social and financial turn of events. As indicated by striking business analyst Lawrence Summers "interest in the instruction of young women likely could be the best yield venture accessible in the creating scene."

## WOMEN IN FINANCIAL AND WORK FIELDS

Women are leaving the boundaries of their homes and joining the job market in the country. There is a visible upward trajectory in the number of women serving in different fields alongside their male counterparts. The quality and quantity, both, are increasing day by day. Women are no less competitive (in some cases, more competitive) than their male counterparts. They are shining in the field of education, healthcare, law, banking, finance, marketing, and administration (receptionists, call centres, typists, secretaries, and fleet management). Some fields (like nursing, teaching, secretarial practice, and marketing) are predominantly female-oriented. Others like law are also witnessing the competency of the female staff. For example, the Supreme Court of India has seen at least eight female judges from Fathima Bibi (1989) to Indira Banerjee (2018). The state is also active in the protection of the female workforce in the country, covering critical areas like job protection, wage disparities, health and safety, maternity leaves, heirship, harassment at the workplace, and exploitation.

## WOMEN IN POLITICAL FIELD

Each nation has the right to have the most ideal pioneer and that implies that women must be given an opportunity to contend. On the off chance that they're never permitted to contend in the constituent cycle, the nations are truly denying themselves of a lot of ability" says Madeleine K. Albright, Chairman of NDI. It is accepted that impartial support of women in legislative issues and government is crucial for construct and support majority rules system. Containing more than 50% of the world's populace, ladies keep on being under-addressed as electors, political pioneers and chose authorities. Majority rule government can't really convey for the entirety of its residents if half of the populace remains underrepresented in the political arena. Every government and the political party must include women in its plans and strategies. Otherwise, they must face the consequences of ignoring half of the population from government, politics, and public administration. Since the bureaucracy and the civil service is in charge of public administration, the representation of women in this area is critical in formulating and implementing the strategies for women in the country. Public administration is the tool of converting public awareness into public policy.

## WOMEN GIVEN EQUIVALENT RIGHTS

10th December 1948 was the defining movement in the history of women equality when the United Nations, through its Resolution # 27A of the General Assembly, declared equal rights for men and women. The apex body took another giant step with the Convention of the Elimination of All Forms of Discrimination Against Women (CEDAW) in 1979. The Convention came into force on 3rd September 1981 after ratification from 189 member states. The Convention defines discrimination and makes it mandatory for the member states to implement a national plan to end the discrimination against women. The Convention characterizes oppression of women in the accompanying terms, "Any differentiation, avoidance or limitation made on the premise of sex which has the impact or motivation behind hindering or invalidating the acknowledgment, satisfaction or exercise by women, regardless of their conjugal status, on a premise of fairness of people, of basic freedoms and basic opportunities in the political, monetary, social, social, common or some other field". The Convention requires the ratifying states to end the discrimination against women in any form (expressed or implied) through a multistep procedure. The first step is the alignment of the legal framework. This step includes defining the discrimination in legal terms, adopting the laws promoting/discouraging the discrimination against women, and abolishing the conflicting laws. The second step is the set up of governing bodies and authorities to implement the legal framework. The final step is the elimination of discrimination from public administration, autonomous bodies, and private institutions. Women should get access to education, health, voting, politics, job opportunities (in the public and private sector), and private life (matrimonial, heirship, citizenship etc.).

## WOMEN IN THE FIELD OF SPORTS

Female support in sports rose drastically in the 20th century, particularly in the last quarter, reflecting changes in current cultures that underlined sex equality. Albeit the degree of investment and execution actually changes significantly by country and by sport have expansive acknowledgment all through the world, and in a couple of examples, for example, figure skating, equal or surpass their male partners in popularity. The primary reason for cooperation of women was to bring fairness between the genders in instructive organizations. Today there are more females taking part in games than any time in recent memory. As of the 2007-2008 school year, females made up 41% of the members in school athletics.

## STRENGTHENING OF WOMEN IN INDIA

The idea of strengthening streams from the force. [54]It is vesting where it doesn't exist or exist deficiently. Strengthening of women would mean preparing women to be financially free, independent, have positive regard to empower them to face any troublesome circumstance and they ought to have the option to partake being developed exercises. The enabled women ought to have the option to take part during the time spent dynamic. In India, the Ministry of Human Resource Development (MHRD1985) and the National Commission for Women(NCW) have been attempted to protect the rights and legitimate privilege of women. The 73rd &74th Amendments (1993) to the constitution of India have given some extraordinary forces to women that for reservation of seats(33%), while the report HRD as March 2002, shows that the governing bodies with the most elevated level of women are, Sweeden 42.7%, Denmark 38%, Findland 36% and Iceland 34.9%. In India "The New Panchayati Raj" is the some portion of the work to engage ladies in any event at the town level. The public authority of India has approved

54. http://www.academicjournal.in/archives/2018/vol3/issue2/3-3-156

different global shows and human rights instruments resolving to tie down equivalent rights to women. The time of 2001 was seen as the time of women strengthening. During the year, a milestone archive has been received, 'the Public Policy for the strengthening of women' For the recipients of the women, the public authority has been embraced various plans and projects for example the National Credit Fund for Women (1993), Food and Nutrition Board (FNB), Information and Mass Education (IMF) and so forth The best improvement most recent couple of years has been the developing contribution of women in the Panchayati Raj foundations. There are many chosen women agents at the town committee level. At present all over India, there are absolute 20, 56, 882 bands Gaon panchayat individuals, out of this women individuals is 8, 38, 244 (40.48%), while absolute Anchalik panchayat [55]individuals is 1, 09, 324, out of this women individuals is 47, 455, (40.41%) and absolute Zila porisod individuals is 11, 708, out of this women individuals is 4, 923 (42.05%). At the focal and state levels too women are logically having an effect. Today we have seen women boss pastors, women president, diverse ideological groups pioneer, well set up money managers and so forth. A considerable lot of them have gone into the making and advertising of a scope of cabin items pickles, fitting, weaving and so on The monetary strengthening of women is being viewed these days as a sine-quo-non of progress for a country; subsequently, the issue of financial strengthening of women is of fundamental significance to political masterminds, social scholars and reformers.

## STATUS OF WOMEN IN MODERN INDIA: INDIAN WOMEN DURING THE NINETEENTH CENTURY

Present day India alludes to the time frame from A.D.1700 to A.D. 1947. In the foundation of the scholarly disturbance of the eighteenth and nineteenth century there was an overall interest for foundation of free and libertarian patriot social orders which

---

55.   http://www.ignited.in/File_upload/79513_39699610.pdf

constantly underlined the balance of women with men. In India, the station request of the general public was tested. Colonization disturbed Indian economy and dislodged the entire segment of craftsmans who began moving to the newly discovered towns and urban communities looking for work in the cutting edge plants. New land income framework denied the provincial and ancestral women of their standard rights to the backwoods, local area property and assets. The proprietorship laws made the conventional farming area an item which can be sold, moved and estranged from the cultivators making another well off working class of zamindars who held hands with the pioneer forces to devastate the laborers. English set up their standard in India, Modernization started in the nineteenth century in India. At the appearance of the British guideline, the situation of ladies in India was at its most minimal ebb. Sati was obviously predominant. Purdah was carefully implemented on Muslim ladies. Moving young ladies had rewarding callings. Practically all the Hindu sanctuaries transparently held devadasis. The British standard, almost certainly, attempted to check every one of these indecencies. The British way of life started to dazzle Indians. The British government found a way intense ways to change the rank ridden Indian social request. There were some illuminated Indians who upheld the British endeavor to change the harsh social request of India. The previously was the annulment of sati by law, on helpful grounds. It was on the fourth December 1892 that the British government in India passed the popular goal by which sati was made a wrongdoing of at fault crime culpable with fine, detainment or both. Raja Ram Mohan Roy addressed the assessment of the illuminated Indian who contended that sati practice had no strict assent. The normal result of the annulment of sati was the acknowledgment of the privilege of the widow to remarriage. The greater part of the change developments (Brahma Samaj of 1825, Prarthana Samaj of 1897 and Arya Samaj of 1875) were driven by male reformers who set the restriction of the opportunity and advancement of ladies. These reformers assaulted just those practices that were very barbarous or obviously savage (obviously influencing just high station Indian ladies). Only sometimes had they tested the connection designs of ladies subjection, sacredness of marriage and family, sexual division of work, and rank chains of command which sustained disparities. women reformers like Pandita Ramabai, Rukhmabai and Tarabai Shinde brought up the inclinations of their contemporary male reformers. Theosophical society was set up at Chennai and Dr. Annie Besant who came from Europe and went along with it. It likewise created general social change program and didn't have an especially sexual orientation agreeable mentality. Cancelation of Sati (widow immolation) of 1829 is viewed as an incredible accomplishment of the reformist development. There is a financial explanation behind the predominance of widow immolation. In Dayabagh framework a widow could acquire property of the sick on the off chance that she has a youngster. Sati successfully forestalls the legacy by widows. The demonstration controlled the 'unlawful' sati and allowed legitimate (sati rehearsed willfully). This guideline turned into an indication of government endorsement of widow immolation prompting real increment of this training. Widow Remarriage was perceived by law in 1856. Widow's remarriage limitation was among high rank and fashionable families. Widow Remarriage was a high station issue, as it was broadly practically speaking among numerous low rank gatherings. Widow's remarriage in levirate structure was usually acknowledged among the Jats of Haryana. In such standard relationships, women only occasionally practiced any dynamic force. The men of the family took such choices regularly against the desire of the women. The new demonstration practically speaking limited the event of widow marriage because of an innate constraint of the demonstration which denied widows any privilege to upkeep or legacy from her better half's property and the kids were to be given over to the family members of her perished spouse. She is placed in a situation of either keeping her youngsters or remarrying. Indeed, even the lower station women needed to deal with the new issue which denied the widows who were remarried of the property acquired from their spouses. Accordingly, after the demonstration was passed less remarriages occurred. Those wedded widows were 'virgin' widows who had no kids to leave behind. Widows who were not virgin widows didn't and couldn't remarry.

## STATUS OF WOMEN IN INDIA: THE TWENTY-FIRST CENTURY

With two decades in the 21st Century already gone, there is no remarkable development in women empowerment in India. Women are still struggling for autonomy to decide about their future. Living in an equivalent country, same society, same culture today they are tormented by the men, they are denied from their own privileges as an individual, they are offended by the man controlled society till now they have not obtain their own position. They have not out from the four dividers after the nightfall, today likewise in a restricted path, in open field, at void field, early afternoon at summer, night in storm, in profound timberland they have been attacking by the male individual from the general public. Since they have a place with female sexual orientation, they are sub-par from the male, they have not the male sex, they are ladies; the "other". As the ladies have not gotten their own genuine situation from the general public even in the second many years of twenty-first century, the subject of sexual orientation value is raised again and this will raise over and over until the sex value will have not basically settled. Society cannot advance in human development index without collaboration between male and female. The collaboration will be sustainable and successful only when it follows the principles of individuality, equality, respect, mutual benefit, dialogue, and commitment. Although the women supposedly safeguard the domestic sphere, they have the mettle of guarding humanity against all the odds (case in point: Durga Devi's battle with the sexist Mahishasura). They do not just conceive an offspring but the incredible political dissident like Subhas Chandra Bose,

Gandhiji, Kshudiram Bose et all; the extraordinary scientist like Inestine, Neoton, Alexander Flemming (Et Al.), extraordinary men like Socretis, Plato, Vidyasagar, Vivekananda, Nietzshe, Barthes, Faucault et everything except likewise contribute a ton to turning out to be them as they are. They have brought up national heroes. They have kept the universe in the balance against all the odds. It is with their efforts that society finds a congenial atmosphere for every member to survive and thrive. History has witnessed such heroics countless times. From the French Revolution to the Nakshalwadi Hamla, the women have protected their societies with their sweat and blood. Yet their efforts are neither acknowledged nor appreciated. They are always seen as ancillary to males. Why should a lady live by a male's personality? The interest of this development ought to be on female own character. The writing quietly moves ladies to such a development against the male power and in India, the brilliant name Arundhati Roy stands separated in her very own class in the field of Women strengthening through writing. Her just one and best novel "Lord of a Small Thing" edifies her movements through the characters like Amu and her mom. They belong to a privileged refined and high society however denied more than the inferior ladies by the social 'restrictions and totems'. Be that as it may, they have not stood these guidelines as their foremothers had withstood. They, at the end of the day, battle against these social authoritative opinions. The extraordinary fire of schooling, Vidyasagar, Vivekanda, Rabindranath Tagore, Raja Rammohon Roy et all had opened the shut entryway of female instruction different hundreds of years prior. They had raised the dark blind and through the open entryway with raising shade the female sexual orientation has reached to the each field and each area of society. Today they are spouses or moms or young ladies, yet they are taught, specialist, well artist, instructor, craftsman of drawing; tune, entertainer, pilot, driver, engineer, specialist, journalist, contender even they are likewise author. They are not just come out from the shut entryway with dark shade they have reached to Mahakas, and Miss Kalpana Chawla is a consistently sublime illustration of that. Every area is fragmented without the ladies. They are courageous women, or principle characters in film world, primary characters in writing, they have place in every conversation. Today isn't just the ladies talk about their basic common freedoms yet in addition the first men of honor have been discussing them. Gone are the days when women were dependent on males to glorify their efforts and to acknowledge their sacrifices. Today's female has the power to touch the sky but the question is: regardless of all these opportunities, have the ladies crossed the half sky and reached to the total sky??? What amount hypothetically they have from the common freedoms; do they have a similar amount an open door in basically??? The inquiry is remained and from one question thousand and thousand inquiries are brought into the world up. One problem conceives thousand issues. Furthermore, that is the reason to get such a lot of chance from basic liberties and opportunity. The ladies today additionally are tormented, separated, denied, pestered, attacked in public space like Park Street (Kolkata), dark alleys, broad day light, bustling tourist spots, religious gatherings, open fields, and even a bus running on the road. Countless events like these, regularly take the headlines of papers only to be forgotten a day later. The torment and attack have not halted till now what begun in Mahabharata as the Kourava attempted to open the garments of Draupadi in the Courtier. Women cry has not halted. They were in some cases stay as Devadasi, sometimes sex manager of jamindar/Mahajan or in some cases when today they have attempted to delete the supposed labels from their gathering, such occurrences have proceeded with in a steady progression.

## CONCLUSION

Women plays a strategic position withinside the society and the economy. The repute of girls in India is rising. The authorities of India, via way of means of passing well timed acts and implementing guidelines and policies looking to empower the women. The impact of women employment on own circle of relatives and society is greater obtrusive in conditions in which girls own better ranges of employment and income. The empowerment of women personnel is likewise better whilst they are at excessive ranges of employment. No doubt, the authorities of India has many guns to tight for women empowerment.

## REFERENCES

1. https://idoc.pub/documents/nadeem-hasnain-indian-society-and-culture-xaamin-vlr02gwkgplz Bottom of Form

2. https://censusindia.gov.in/Data_Products/Library/Provisional_Population_Total_link/PDF_Links/chapter6.pdf

3. Indian Society Themes and Social Issues by Nadeem Hasnain.

# 6

# RAPE

## ABSTRACT

Rape is among the most elevated types of wrongdoing experienced by ladies on the whole areas of the society. As of late, there has been a disturbing ascent in proportion of assault in India.. Delhi sacked the questionable record of being the lone association region where such violations were accounted for. Assault is a genuine wrongdoing and progressively acquiring perceivability as a significant general wellbeing concern. The present study intended to discover the segment profile of assault casualties and the effect of assault. An aggregate of 100 assault casualties from cover homes and various regions of Delhi were taken as the example of the investigation. A casual meeting was led to acquire, a general photos of casualty's horrible experience. A contextual analysis approach was continued in surveying for casualties injury caused by assault and different affronts. Data was gotten from the casualties verbal and conduct correspondences. Subtleties relating to age, religion, proficiency, Socio-financial status, conjugal status, site of rate, number of attackers, and relationship with aggressors were noted down. It was tracked down that a large portion of the casualties were ignorant or inadequately instructed, unmarried and had a place with the lower social portions of the general public. Exceptionally influenced age bunch was 11-15 yrs. In larger part of the cases casualty knew the attacker. Countless invalid consensual assault cases has been noted down. The home of the casualty was the most normally noted area of rape. Casualties likewise announced that they face social shame, shame and endure genuine blame aches on the off chance that they register for fight. It's extremely hard to request help on the grounds that the assault has caused them to feel embarrassed, powerless, and injured.

KEYWORDS- Indian Penal Code 1860, Sexual Violence, Crime

## INTRODUCTION

India is basically recognized as one of the most capable country as compare to other countries. The varied and teenage population dividend provides acceleration to the greater possibility of much better future for the country. Gradually, India is improving in all related features of the growth but between all these things, there is something which keeps troubling the scholars and makes them rethink related to the social and geographical framework of our nation. The gradual increase rate of crime against women in India has emerged as one of the biggest issue in the nation which government faced now-a-days. It is very essential to handle or manage the sexual assault against the females.

During the old time Indian women held a high spot of regard in the general public as referenced in Rig-veda and different scriptures. However, later on, as a result of social, political and economic changes, women lost their status and were consigned to the foundation (Crime against women, 2013). The authority insights showed a declining sex-proportion, wellbeing status, education rate, work investment rate and political support among women. While then again the spread of social indecencies like endowment deaths, youngster marriage, abusive behavior at home, assault, sexual badgering, misuse of women laborers are widespread in various parts of India. Embarrassment, assault, kidnapping, attack, share death, torment, wife-beating and so forth have grown up throughout the long term (Singh and

Choudhury, 2012). "Crime" is an exceptionally basic word that goes over in everyday life. "The Semantic meaning of 'crime against women' is immediate or circuitous physical or mental pitilessness to Girls and women's. Crimes which are coordinated explicitly against women and in which just women are casualties are described as "Crime against Women".

It is similarly essential to explain the idea of 'Violence against women'. Violence is otherwise called misuse and incorporates such an actual hostility or gets rowdy. Fighting violence against women requires testing the way that sex jobs and force relations are verbalized towards women will take quite a while at some point it happens one age to future. As per one investigation around 30% children are experienced different sort sexual maltreatment, for example, making a youngster rub private parts, making a kid disclosure private parts being captured naked and so forth (Derby, 2013). A lawful assumption was likewise made against the blamed in cases for custodial assault, if the lady asserted that the demonstration was without her assent. Inspite of these change instances of assault is showing their upward pattern (Khandelwal, 2015). The quantity of assault cases increment because of impact of broad communications openness. At times subsequent to watching motion pictures and getting thought individuals get include in sexual violence, portrayal of crime and brutality, battling scenes, foul language and romance Films becomes hit due to no nonsense assault and assault scenes taking all things together the subtleties.

Sexual violence against lady represents an on edge circumstance, for Indian specialists. Lately, every one of the legislatures have zeroed in on, the expanding number of crimes against lady and appear to be concerned, by the volcanic development in the numbers. As indicated by reports distributed in Times of India (2008), assault is the quickest developing crime in India. In the previous few years, the report from service proposes that, India remains at the third position, on the crimes against lady. Here, the examination centers around the assault cases that are accounted for, the exploration does exclude the quantity of cases which are not announced. As per sources just 10% of the assault cases, are accounted for and rest 90% of the cases go unreported, because of a few individual and social reasons. The momentum research concentrates on the diverse segment factors that are vital in detailing the assault cases. The examination remembers three central point for the investigation, separately proficiency rate, populace thickness and sex proportion.

## SEXUAL VIOLENCE: THE GLOBAL SCENARIO

An investigation by the World Health Organization (2005) proposes that, one out of each five women have confronted either assault or an endeavored assault, once in the course of her life. The examination additionally depicts that in Canada, United Kingdom and United States, 15% of the lady has confronted the sexual violence, while South Africa was accounted for as the weakest country, with 40% of the lady announced Violence.

## SEXUAL VIOLENCE IN INDIA

The status of lady in Indian culture, has seen a steady decay. The women of pre-vedic period were given equivalent rights, and were dealt with similarly as man, from there on; the decrease in the status of lady in Indian culture proceeds (Halli and Mullal, 2016). The social and social construction of India, has consistently subjected lady, and the overall set of laws has consistently thought about them as frail and latent, which really works as an instrument for subjection of lady (Cossman and Kapur, 2002). The male centric outlook powers lady to a simple circumstance, where they feel perilous and helpless against their male counterparts (Kapur, 1996).

Violence against lady incorporates a wide range of gendered crimes like boisterous attack, sexual maltreatment, sexual attack and actual violence (Merry, 2009). Here in the ebb and flow research paper the point of convergence is to comprehend the components of segment variables and its effect on sexual violence against lady. Among all types of sexual violence, assault is viewed as the most gendered forceful demonstration, towards the lady (Ignatuis, 2013).

The word assault is started from a Latin word 'rapere', which alludes to 'unlawful sexual action'. There are a few episodes detailed in our folklores, now and again and assault is considered as a deplorable crime from the antiquated occasions. One such model is from the epic Ramayana, where Ravana carried out this crime to a divine sprite Rambha, at that point her significant other Nalkubar reviled him that, the second he contacts a lady without wanting to, his head will part into seven pieces. The previously mentioned model shows that, even the most influential individuals can't stay away from the discipline, of this terrible crime.

The view of assault shifts from one culture to another; particularly in Indian situation, assault is considered as stigmatic and horrendous, for the people in question (Madan and Sinha, 2013). In Indian situation assault casualties feel damaged just as, it is one of only a handful few crimes, where the victim is being criticized by the general public. This insight towards the casualties is likewise characteristic of the man centric nature of the Indian culture. In spite of the fact that India has accomplished opportunity in 1947, the lady in India actually required the freedom and strengthening. In the previous few years our nation has seen a volcanic development in assault cases being accounted for, there might be a few reasons that may clarify the explanation of the assault cases detailed.

## RAPE

United Nations included assault, under the sexual violence against lady. It characterizes sex based violence as a demonstration of prompting physical, social or mental mischief, to a lady. The other meaning of assault incorporates, any sexual demonstration against the desire of the person in question (Smith, 1998). Assault isn't only a fanatical craving of sexual satisfaction, yet generally in the public eye, it is being drilled by the man, to set up the prevalence over the lady (Goonesekere, 2004). In India, assault has destroying results on the casualty's life, there are many negative responses, and social disgrace is joined to it (Karmen, 2010). Aside from social and social seclusion, casualties of assault become defenseless against a few physical and mental issues. The casualties may fall prey to a few infections, as STIs and HIV/AIDS after the attack. The casualties may likewise encounter mental issues like nervousness, dread and posttraumatic problem (Mcanulty and Burnette, 2006).

## LITERATURE REVIEW

The word 'crime against women' has gotten a "quiet scourge", with an ever increasing number of instances of assault, attack and sexual attack being accounted for from school grounds, while struggling and working environments. "It's an extremely mind boggling issue, including legitimate, social and mental angles (Rufus, 2014). Women in metropolitan regions are twice pretty much as likely as men to encounter violence, especially in non-industrial nations (Vanderschueren, 2000). Concurring United Kingdom's little girl narrative 2015, UK is the fifth spot at the world's assault list, in consistently 250 women of UK are getting assault, the examinations shows that men who submitting assault comes from each economic, ethnic and gathering of people

Across the world women's are confronting significant crime of 'assault and sexual provocation and so forth, Johnson have portrayed about assault cases in USA for example no other significant classification of crime not homicide, attack or theft has generated a more genuine test of the validity of public crime measurements than assault (Taylor et al., 2007). Universally, assault is infrequently detailed by young ladies and women's because of the intense social, religion and rank shame or the dread of reject by their relatives or exposed to violence and where early sex are unlawful, or early sex can confront indictment under the laws (Harter, 2011). Assault is a notoriously under-announced crime in India. Since survivors of assault can confront arraignment under the current laws, as per these laws they need to confront protracted indictment and examination. In the event that there is no adequate proof to demonstrate an assault in the court they can't get equity, even after the ventured the court. During examination casualties may show that they were a not virgin which isn't permitted to get marriage in the general public.

As indicated by Indian express dated on 15th Dec 2013, National Crime Records Bureau of India uncovers that there has been an eight-overlap expansion in the quantity of assaults over the most recent forty years. The ascent in the quantity of assault cases is the most quick contrasted with other genuine crimes like homicide, theft and kidnapping (Sardar, 2013). For each 60 minutes, 2.84 instances of assault were accounted for in country in which, on a normal, 3.55 people were captured during the year 2012 (NCRB, 2012). JAGORI and UN Women report 2010 have tracked down that, In New Delhi around 66% of women's accounted for encountering sexual badgering between two to multiple times during the previous year (JAGORI and Women, 2010). Assault cases step by step expansion in significant urban areas India. For the most part individuals accept that the essential driver of assault is a forceful longing to rule the casualty as opposed to an endeavor to accomplish sexual satisfaction (JAGORI and Women, 2010). The one assault and killed case were occurred in Delhi (16 Dec. 2012) Capital of India with 23 years of age young lady. The young lady was going in transport with her male companion, and another six man additionally going in a similar transport. In moving transport, abruptly each of the six man have get forceful and beaten her male companion and doing assaulted with her including transport driver. After procured of young lady they have through her side of street. The young lady was passed on from her virginal wounds following thirteen days going through crisis treatment in Singapore.

## CONCLUSION

Sexual violence against lady in India is rising and depicts, the troubling picture towards the general public, and various establishments. Furthermore, everybody needs to make some particular and powerful move, against individuals who are perpetrating these sorts of crime. The snappy and productive arraignment, which guarantees the conveyance of equity on schedule, will be viable in diminishing these sorts of crime, against the lady. The general public ought to likewise chip away at reshaping its point of view, towards the young lady, and they ought to be given greater security and legitimate consideration towards them.

## REFERENCES

1.  Cossman, Brenda, and RatnaKapur. 2002. Secularism's Last Sigh: Hindutva and the (Mis)Rule of Law. Delhi, India: Oxford University Press.

2.  Kapur, Ratna, and Brenda Cossman. 1996. Subversive Sites: Feminist Engagements with Law in India. New Delhi, India: Sage Publications.s

3.  Smith, Merril D., ed., Sex and Sexuality in Early America. New York: New York University Press, 1998. This collection contains original essays on sex and sex-related issues in early America. Several of the essays focus on rape and sexual coercion.

4.  Goonesekere, Savitri (2004) Violence, Law and Women's Rights in South Asia, SAGE Publications-India.

5. Karmen, Andrew (2010) Crime Victims: An Introduction to Victimology, Seventh edition, Wadsworth Cengage Learning.

6. Smith, Merril D. (2004) Encyclopedia of Rape, Greenwood Press-US

7. Mcanulty, Richard D; Burnette, Mary Michele (2006) Sex and Sexuality: Sexual deviation and sexual offenses. Exhibitionism, Volume three, Greenwood Publishing Group, Inc.

8. Arun Ignatius,(2013). Sexual Violence in India.

9. (2014). Crime in India. Compedium of Crime, GOI.

10. Armed Forces Department Corp. (2005). Woman in an Insecure World. Geneva: WHO.

11. Madan V K & Sinha R K (2013). The Dynamics of Rape in Modern Indian Society. International Journal of Juridical Sciences, 81-87.

12. Mullal, C. H. (2016). Status Of Women In India" Status Of Ancient, Mediaeval And Modern. Imperial Journal of Interdisciplinary Research.

13. Shakya T M, Dangal. G. (2014). Marital Rape and its Social Demographic factors associated with Gynecological problems in Kirtipur. Nepal Journal of Obstetrics and Gynaecology, 64-69.

14. Crime against women 2013. Loke Sabha Secretariat, Parliament library and reference research documentation and information services, reference no. 2/RN/Ref./2013.

15. Derby, J. 2013. On rape, from silence to justice. The Hindu, 15 June 2013.

16. Dreze, J. and Khera, R. 2000. Crime, gender, and society in India: Insights from homicide data. Population and Development Review, 26(2), 335-352.

17. Guruappa, N. 2011. Violence against Women in India. Serials Publications, New Delhi, p. 23.

18. Harter, P. 2011. Libya rape victims face honor killings. BBC News Libya rape victims 'face honor killings. http://www.bbc.com/news/world-africa-13760895.

19. Hilberman, E. 1978. The impact of rape. In The woman patient (pp. 303-322). Springer US.

20. JAGORI and Women, U.N. 2010. Report on the Baseline Survey.http://jagori.org/wp-content/uploads/2011/03/Baseline-Survey_layout_for-Print_06_04_2015.pdf.

21. Khandelwal, S. K. 2015. A Socio legal Study of Crimes Against Women A Critical Review of Protective Laws.

22. Koss, M. P., Goodman, L. A., Browne, A., Fitzgerald, L. F., Keita, G. P. and Russo, N. F. 1994. No safe haven: Male violence against women at home, at work, and in the community. American Psychological Association.

23. Sardar, K. 2013. A year after Nirbhaya, rapid rise in number of rape complaints. The new Indian express. http://www.newindianexpress.com/thesundaystandard/A-Year-After-Nirbhaya-Rapid-Rise-in-Number-of-Rape-Complaints/2013/12/15/article1946075.ece

24. Singh, A.K. and Choudhury, A. 2012. Violence against Women and Children-Issues and Concerns. Serials Publications, New Delhi.

25. Singh, S. R. 2014. Incest rapes in Delhi up, fathers among offenders. Hindustan Times 19, Nov, 2014. New Delhi.

26. Taylor Jr, S., Johnson, K. C. and Johnson, R. D. 2007. Until proven innocent: Political correctness and the shameful injustices of the Duke lacrosse rape case. Macmillan.

27. The Economic Times 2012. Delhi gang rape: Protests go viral nationwide, unstoppable public outpouring as gang rape victim dies, New Delhi, 30, December.

28. The Telegraph 2012. (2012-12-19). Video: Protests grow over gang rape of Indian woman. 19, Dec 2012, London.

# 7

# A STUDY ON ISSUES AND CHALLENGES OF WOMEN EMPOWERMENT IN MODERN INDIA

## ABSTRACT

This paper endeavors to break down the situation with Women Empowerment in India and features the Issues and Challenges of Women Empowerment. Today the strengthening of ladies has gotten perhaps the main worries of 21$^{st}$ century. Be that as it may, for all intents and purposes ladies strengthening is as yet a figment of the real world. We see in our everyday life how ladies become misled by different social shades of malice. Ladies Empowerment is the crucial instrument to extend ladies' capacity to have assets and to settle on essential life decisions. Strengthening of ladies is basically the cycle of upliftment of financial, social and political status of ladies, the customarily oppressed ones, in the general public. It is the way toward guarding them against all types of savagery. The investigation depends on absolutely from optional sources. The examination uncovers that ladies of India are generally debilitated and they appreciate to some degree lower status than that of men notwithstanding numerous endeavors embraced by Government. It is discovered that acknowledgment of inconsistent sexual orientation standards by ladies are as yet winning in the general public. The investigation finishes up by a perception that admittance to Education, Employment and Change in Social Structure are just the empowering variables to Women Empowerment. Catchphrases: Women Empowerment, Education, Health, Socio-Economic Status. Wrongdoings against ladies, Policy implications. [56]Financial Inclusion is viewed as a basic marker for improvement and prosperity of the general public all throughout the planet. Offering comprehensive monetary types of assistance, that is, monetary administrations moderate for all, has become an essential need in numerous nations including India. G-20 Nations have accentuated on monetary consideration as a facilitator for accomplishing sexual orientation fairness and other feasible improvement objectives. Ladies strengthening is an extreme methodology worried about changing force relations for female sex and thought about fundamental for worldwide advancement. Accordingly, a comprehensive monetary model is being embraced in non-industrial countries to accomplish essential to developmental targets. The current article examines the elements of ladies strengthening, that is, social, political, and monetary. It additionally embraces a test to check whether the measurements change with monetary consideration. The creators attract upon writing to build up an organized poll on ladies strengthening and monetary incorporation through plans like Pradhan Mantri Jan Dhan Yojana (PMJDY), Pradhan Mantri Jivan Jyoti Bima Yojana (PMJJBY), Pradhan Mantri Suraksha Bima Yojana (PMSBY), and Atal Pension Yojana (APY) on ladies living in metropolitan ghettos in the mechanical town of Ludhiana, Punjab. The information were gathered from 737 females living in metropolitan ghettos with PMJDY financial balances. The outcome showed that PMJDY plot has been very fruitful particularly in the event of ladies in ghettos and affects social, political, and financial elements of ladies strengthening. The investigation adds to existing writing by propelling the discussion on ladies in metropolitan ghettos and

---

56.   https://journals.sagepub.com/doi/full/10.1177/0256090919897809.

recognizes the significant requirement for the improvement of formal monetary framework to upgrade the size of monetary consideration.

KEYWORDS- Constitution of India, Women and Child, Gender Based, Women Rights

## INTRODUCTION

Ladies strengthening alludes to expanding the otherworldly, political, social, instructive, sex or monetary strength of people and networks of ladies. Ladies' strengthening in India is vigorously subject to a wide range of factors that incorporate topographical area (metropolitan/provincial) instructive status social status (standing and class) and age. Approaches on Women's strengthening exist at the public, state and neighborhood (Panchayat) levels in numerous areas, including wellbeing, instruction, monetary freedoms, sex based viciousness what's more, political support. Anyway there are huge hole between strategy headways and genuine practice at the local area level. Strengthening of ladies is basically the cycle of upliftment of financial, social and political status of ladies, the customarily oppressed ones, in the general public. It is the way toward guarding them against all types of savagery. Ladies strengthening includes the structure up of a general public, a world of politics, wherein ladies can inhale without the dread of abuse, misuse, worry, segregation and the general sensation of abuse which goes with being a lady in a customarily male overwhelmed structure.

Ladies comprise practically half of the total populace yet India has shown unbalanced sex proportion whereby female's populace has been nearly lower than guys. To the extent their societal position is concerned, they are not treated as equivalent to men taking all things together the spots. In the Western social orders, the ladies have equivalent right and status with men taking all things together different backgrounds. In any case, sex inabilities and separations are found in India indeed, even today. The incomprehensible circumstance has with the end goal that she was now and then worried as Goddess and at different occasions simply as slave.

## REVIEW OF LITERATURE

H. Subrahmanyam (2011) thinks about ladies training in India as of now and Past. Creator featured that there has a decent advancement in generally enrolment of young lady understudies in schools. The term enable intends to give legitimate force or position to act. It is the way toward obtaining a few exercises of ladies.

M. Bhavani Sankara Rao (2011) has featured that strength of ladies individuals from SHG have unquestionably taken a go to better. It obviously shows that heath of ladies individuals examine among themselves about wellbeing related issues of different individuals and their youngsters and make them mindful of different Government arrangements exceptionally implied for them. Doepke M. Tertilt M. (2011) Does Female Empowerment Promote Economic Development? This investigation is an observational investigation recommending that cash in the possession of moms benefits kids. This examination built up a arrangement of non agreeable family bartering models to comprehend what sort of contacts can bring about the noticed experimental relationship.[57]

Duflo E. (2011) Women's Empowerment and Economic Development, National Bureau of Economic Research Cambridge The study argues that the inter relationships of the Empowerment and Development are probably too weak to be self sustaining and that continuous policy commitment to equally for its own sake may be needed to bring about equality between men and women.

---

57. http://iosrjournals.org/iosr-jbm/papers/Vol17-issue4/Version-1/B017411319.pdf.

Sethuraman K. (2008) The Role of Women's Empowerment and Domestic Violence in child Growth and Under nutrition in a Tribal and Rural Community in South India. This research paper explores the relationship between Women's Empowerment and Domestic Violence, maternal nutritional status and the nutritional status and growth over six months in children aged 6 to 24 months in a rural and tribal community. This longitudinal observational study undertaken in rural Karnataka. India included tribal and rural subjects. Venkata Ravi and Venkatraman (2005) focused on the effects of SHG on women participation and exercising control over decision making both in family matters and in group activities.

## OBJECTIVES OF THE STUDY

1.  To know the need of Women Empowerment.

2.  To evaluate the Awareness of Women Empowerment in India.

3.  To investigate the Factors affecting the Economic Empowerment of Women.

4.  To read the Government Schemes For Women Empowerment.

5.  To distinguish the Hindrances in the Path of Women Empowerment.

6.  To submit valuable Ideas in the light of Findings.

## RESEARCH METHODOLOGY

This paper is fundamentally spellbinding and insightful in nature. In this paper an endeavor has been taken to investigate the strengthening of in India. The information utilized in it is simply from optional sources as indicated by the need of this examination.

## CURRENT SITUATION OF WOMEN

New Delhi: Being equivalent to their male partners is as yet a long ways for Indian ladies. Not exclusively are they minimal as well known people a normal Indian ladies can scarcely make major decisions at home or outside. In 2012, ladies involved just 8 out of 74 ecclesiastical situations in the association committee of pastors. There were just 2 ladies decided out of 26 adjudicators in the Supreme Court and there were just 54 ladies decided out of 634 appointed authorities in different high courts.

### STUNNING FACTS:

As per 2013, UNDP report on Human Development Indicators, all south Asian Countries with the exception of Afghanistan, were positioned preferred for ladies over India It predicts: an Indian young lady kid matured 1-5 years is 75% bound to bite the dust than the kid. A ladies is assaulted once in each 20 min and 10% of all violations are detailed. Ladies structure 48% of India's Population, just 29% of the National labor force, just 26% ladies have admittance to formal credit.

## WHY NEED OF WOMEN EMPOWERMENT?

Reflecting into the "Vedas Purana" of Indian culture, ladies is being venerated like LAXMI

MAA, goddess of riches; SARSWATI MAA, for intelligence; DURGA MAA for influence. The situation with ladies in India especially in rustic territories needs to address the issue of enabling ladies. About 66% of the female populace in rustic territory is unutilized. This is mostly because of existing social traditions. In farming and Animal care the ladies contribute 90% of the all out labor force. Ladies establish practically 50% of the populace, perform almost 2/3 of its work hours, get 1/tenth of the world's pay and own under 1/100th the world property. Among the world's 900 million unskilled individuals, ladies out number men two to one. 70% of individuals living in neediness are ladies. Lower sex proportion for example 933, The current examinations show that the ladies are generally less solid than men however have a place with same class. They establish under 1/seventh of the executives and troughs in non-industrial nations. Just 10% seats in World Parliament and 6% in National Cabinet are held by ladies.

## [58]HINDRANCES OF WOMEN EMPOWERMENT

The main Problems that were faced by women in past days and still today up to some extent:

1. Gender discrimination

2. Lack of Education

3. Female Infanticide

4. Financial Constraints

5. Family Responsibility

6. Low Mobility

7. Low ability to bear Risk

8. Low need for achievement

9. Absence of ambition for the achievement Social status Dowry Marriage in same caste and child marriage (still existing) Atrocities on Women (Raped, Kicked, Killed, Subdued, humiliated almost daily.)

## [59]WAYS TO EMPOWER WOMEN

1. Changes in women's mobility and social interaction

2. Changes in women's labour patterns

58. http://iosrjournals.org/iosr-jbm/papers/Vol17-issue4/Version-1/ B017411319.pdf
59. http://iosrjournals.org/iosr-jbm/papers/Vol17-issue4/Version-1/ B017411319.pdf

3. Changes in women's access to and control over resources

4. Changes in women's control over Decision making Providing education Self employment and

5. Self help group Providing minimum needs like Nutrition, Health, Sanitation, Housing Other than this society should change the mentality towards the word women Encouraging women to develop in their fields they are good at and make a career.

## [60]GOVERNMENT SCHEMES FOR WOMEN EMPOWERMENT

The Government programmes for women development began as early as 1954 in India but the actual participation began only in 1974. At present, the Government of India has over 34 schemes for women operated by different department and ministries. Some of these are as follows;

1. Rastria Mahila Kosh (RMK) 1992-1993

2. Mahila Samridhi Yojana (MSY) October, 1993.

3. Indira Mahila Yojana (IMY) 1995.

4. Women Entrepreneur Development programme given top priority in 1997-98.

5. Mahila Samakhya being implemented in about 9000 villages.

6. Swayasjdha.

7. Swa Shakti Group.

8. Support to Training and Employment Programme for Women(STEP).

9. Swalamban.

---

60. http://iosrjournals.org/iosr-jbm/papers/Vol17-issue4/Version-1/ B017411319.pdf

10. Crèches/ Day care centre for the children of working and ailing mother.

11. Hostels for working women.

12. Swadhar.

13. National Mission for Empowerment of Women.

14. Integrated Child Development Services (ICDS) (1975),

15. Rajiv Gandhi Scheme for Empowerment of Adolescence Girls (RGSEAG) (2010).

16. The Rajiv Gandhi National Crèche Scheme for Children of Working Mothers.

17. Integrated Child Protection scheme (ICPS) (2009-2010).

18. Dhanalakahmi (2008).

19. Short Stay Homes.

20. Ujjawala (2007).

21. Scheme for Gender Budgeting (XI Plan).

22. Integrated Rural Development Programme (IRDP).

23. Training of Rural Youth for Self Employment (TRYSEM).

24. Prime Minister's Rojgar Yojana (PMRY).

25. Women's Development Corporation Scheme (WDCS).

26. Working Women's Forum.

27. Indira Mahila Kendra.

28. Mahila Samiti Yojana.

29. Khadi and Village Industries Commission.

30. Indira Priyadarahini Yojana.

31. SBI's Sree Shaki Scheme.

32. SIDBI's Mahila Udyam Nidhi Mahila Vikas Nidhi.

33. NGO's Credit Schemes.

34. National Banks for Agriculture and Rural Development's Schemes

The efforts of government and its different agencies are ably supplemented by nongovernmental organizations that are playing an equally important role in facilitating women empowerment. Despite concerted efforts of governments and NGOs there are certain gaps. Of course we have come a long way in empowering women yet the future journey is difficult and demanding.

## STATUS OF WOMEN EMPOWERMENT

The situation with Women Empowerment can't be imagined with single measurement rather multidimensional appraisal as far as different parts of ladies' life and their status would bring a clear origination. Along these lines, this paper attempts to give a fundamental thought regarding the condition and status of ladies as far as business, instruction, wellbeing and societal position.. India acquired eight spots (from 113 position in 2011 to 105 position in 2012) because of progress in the instructive achievements and political strengthening. Keeping to the side the Political Empowerment, the other three lists is all over the position of 100. The Political Empowerment positions very high might be because of the 73rd and 74th Constitution corrections of India giving more noteworthy freedom to ladies to participate in dynamic governmental issues.

## EXPLANATIONS BEHIND THE EMPOWERMENT OF WOMEN

Today we have seen various Acts and Schemes of the focal Government just as state Government to engage the ladies of India. In any case, in India ladies are segregated and minimized at each level of the general public whether it is social interest, political investment, monetary support, admittance to training, and furthermore regenerative medical care. Ladies are discovered to be financially extremely helpless everywhere on the India.

A couple of ladies are occupied with administrations and different exercises. Thus, they need financial ability to remain all alone legs on per with men. Other hand, it has been seen that ladies are discovered to be less educated than men. As per 2001 registration, pace of proficiency among men in India is discovered to be 76% while it is as it were 54% among ladies. Hence, expanding schooling among ladies is of vital in engaging them. It has additionally saw that some of ladies are too powerless to even consider working. They devour less food however work more. Subsequently, from the wellbeing perspective, ladies society who are to be more vulnerable are to be made more grounded. Another issue is that work environment badgering of ladies. There are such countless instances of assault, grabbing of young lady, share badgering, thus on. Thus, they require strengthening of different sorts to ensure themselves and to get their immaculateness and pride. To summarize, ladies strengthening can not be conceivable except if ladies accompany and help to self-enable themselves. There is a need to plan diminishing feminized neediness, advancing training of ladies, and anticipation and disposal of savagery against ladies.

## CHALLENGES

There are a few imperatives that check the interaction of ladies strengthening in India. Normal practices and family structure in non-industrial nations like India, shows and sustain the subordinate status of ladies. One of the standards is the proceeding with inclination for a child over the introduction of a young lady youngster which in present in nearly all social orders and networks. The general public is more one-sided for male kid in regard of training, sustenance and different freedoms. The underlying driver of this sort of mentality lies in the conviction that male kid acquires the faction in India with a special case of Meghalaya. Ladies frequently disguise the conventional idea of their job as normal in this manner incurring an unfairness upon them. Destitution is the truth of life for by far most ladies in India. It is the another factor that stances challenge in understanding ladies' strengthening. There are a few difficulties that are tormenting the issues of ladies' privilege in India. Focusing on these issues will straightforwardly profit the strengthening of ladies in India Schooling: While the nation has developed from a far cry since freedom where instruction is concerned. the hole among ladies and men is extreme. While 82.14% of grown-up men are instructed, as it were 65.46% of grown-up ladies are known to be proficient in India. The sex predisposition is in advanced education, particular expert trainings which hit ladies hard in work and accomplishing top administration in any field.

a. Education: Poverty is viewed as the best danger to harmony on the planet, and destruction of destitution ought to be a public objective as significant as the destruction of lack of education. Because of this, ladies are misused as homegrown makes a difference.

b. Wellbeing and Safety: The wellbeing and security worries of ladies are principal for the prosperity of a country furthermore, is a significant factor in measuring the strengthening of ladies in a country. Anyway there are disturbing concerns where maternal medical care is concerned.

c. Proficient Inequality: This imbalance is polished in work sand advancements. Ladies face endless impediment in male tweaked and overwhelmed environs in Government Offices and Private undertakings.

d. Profound quality and Inequality: Due to sex inclination in wellbeing and sustenance there is uncommonly high profound quality rate in ladies decreasing their populace further particularly in Asia, Africa and china.

e. Family Inequality: Household relations show sex inclination in imperceptibly little yet critical habits all over the globe, all the more along these lines, in India for example sharing weight of housework, childcare and modest works by supposed division of work.

## CONSTITUTIONAL PROVISIONS ON WOMEN EMPOWERMENT

1. Constitutional Provisions For Empowering Women In India Equality before law for all persons (Article-14).

2. Prohibition of discrimination on grounds of religion, race, caste, sex or place of birth (Article 15(I)).

3. However, special provisions may be made by the state in favors of women and children Article 15(3).

4. Equality of opportunity for all citizens relating to employment or appointment to any office under the state (Article 16).

5. State policy to be directed to securing for men and women equally the right to an adequate means of livelihood (Article 39(a);

6. (v) equal pay for equal work for both men and women (Article 39(d).

7. Provisions to be made by the state for securing just and humane conditions of work and maternity relief (Article 42).

8. Promotion of harmony by every citizen of India and renouncement of such practices which are derogatory to the dignity of women Article 51A(e).

9.  Reservation of not less than one-third of total seats for women in direct election to local bodies, viz; Panchayats and Municipalities (Articles 343(d) and 343 (T).

## CONCLUSION

Consequently, the accomplishment in the field of pay/business and in instructive front, the situation of ladies strengthening is by all accounts similarly poor. The need of great importance is to distinguish those escape clauses or impediments which are noticing the acknowledgment of strengthening of ladies and this activity should be begun from the ladies people itself just as more critically strategy activity taken by the state and society. Let us make the vow that we need a populist society where everyone whether men or ladies get the equivalent freedom to communicate and elevate one's prosperity and prosperity of the general public as entirety.

Ladies' strengthening is certainly not a Northern idea ladies everywhere on the world, remembering nations for South, have been testing and changing sexual orientation disparities since the start of the set of experiences. "At the point when ladies push ahead the family moves, the town moves and the country moves". It is fundamental as their suspected and their worth frameworks lead the improvement of a decent family, great society and eventually a decent country. The most ideal method of strengthening is maybe through accepting ladies in the standard of improvement. Ladies strengthening will be genuine and viable just when they are supplied pay and property with the goal that they may remain on their feet and develop their personality in the general public. The Empowerment of Women has gotten perhaps the main worries of 21$^{st}$ century not just at public level yet additionally at the global level. Government activities alone would not be adequate to accomplish this objective. Society should step up to the plate and establish an environment where there is no sex segregation and ladies have full chances of self dynamic and taking part in friendly, political and monetary existence of the country with a feeling of fairness.

## REFERENCES

1. Duflo E. (2011) Women's Empowerment and Economic Development, National Bureau of Economic Research, Cambridge.

2. India: Women's Empowerment - IFAD/OE, 2000. The Republic of India; TamiluNadu Women's Development Project: Completion Evaluation, Report 340 – IN Rome, April.

3. Baruah B. (2013) Role of Electronic Media in Empowering Rural.

4. Goswami, L. (2013). Education for Women Empowerment. ABHIBYAKTI: Annual Journal, 1, 17-18.

5. Baruah, B. (2013). Role of Electronic Media in Empowering Rural Women Education of N.E. India. ABHIBYAKTI: Annual Journal, 1, 23-26.

6. Kadam, R. N. (2012). Empowerment of Women in India- An Attempt to Fill the Gender Gap. International Journal of Scientific and Research Publications, 2(6), 11-13.

7. Nagaraja, B. (2013). Empowerment of Women in India: A Critical Analysis. Journal of Humanities and Social Science (IOSRJHSS), 9(2), 45-52 [WWW page]. URL http: www. Iosrjournals.Org/empowerment.html.

8. Deshpande, S., and Sethi, S., (2010). Role and Position of Women Empowerment in Indian Society. International Referred Research Journal, 1(17), 10-12.

9. Kishor, S. and Gupta, K. (2009), Gender Equality and Women's Empowerment in India, NATIONAL FAMILY HEALTH SURVEY (NFHS-3) INDIA, 2005-06,

International Institute for Population Sciences, Deonar, Mumbai.

10. Suguna, M., (2011). Education and Women Empowerment in India. ZENITH: International Journal of Multidisciplinary Research, 1(8), 19-21.

11. Dr. Dasarati Bhuyan "Empowerment of Indian Women: A challenge of 21st Century" Orissa Review, 2006

12. Vinze, Medha Dubashi (1987) "Women Empowerment of Indian: A Socio Economic study of Delhi" Mittal Publications, Delhi..

13. Dhruba Hazarika "Women Empowerment in India: a Brief Discussion" International Journal of Educational Planning & Administration. Volume 1, Number 3 (2011)

14. Pankaj Kumar Baro1 & Rahul Sarania "Employment and Educational Status: Challenges of Women Empowerment in India", A Peer-Reviewed Indexed International Journal of Humanities & Social Science.

15. http://www.slideshare.net/puneetsharma5688/women-empowermentpuneet-sharma.

# 8

# DOWRY DEATH: A VIOLATION OF THE RIGHT TO LIFE AND LEGAL PROTECTION OF WOMEN IN INDIA

## ABSTRACT

Dowry Death might be a consuming issue of the Indian culture since years. The unnatural demise of new hitched young woman on account of endowment is normal title text of every paper. Security of youthful hitched ladies' against badgering and savagery because of share is duty of state. Boycott of giving and taking settlement - the share Prohibition Act, 1961, is that the one that is most commonly tested since its beginning wherever the country. To impact this segment 304B (Dowry passings) and 498 - A (Cruelty by spouse or - laws) were joined inside the Indian board code inside the center 1980's. Improvement of instructional remaining of females by instructional mindfulness programs close by extreme disciplines to wrongdoers are helpful to impact this social mongrels.

Marriage is an essential bit of society, a wellspring of rapture and good times and furthermore of new beginnings. In any case, one of the longest standing shades of noxiousness related with marriage from a woman's point of view in the Indian culture is the Dowry system. Despite an extraordinary bargain being said and done against the custom, it is at this point inescapable in the 21st century, in both subtle and clear ways. The establishment of a huge gathering of social shocks against women, the custom of presenting blessing is the crudest enunciation of the male-transcendence in the overall population. It is consistently the mandatory custom of a youngster's people giving a parcel of cash, gold as diamonds, electronic stuff, versatile or passionate properties, to the plan and his family, at the period of marriage. Despite the way that the beginning stage of the custom lies with gatekeepers endeavoring to ensure budgetary adequacy for their daughters, in current perspective it has changed over into gatekeepers settling up for the assertion of thriving of their young ladies. The decorations and cash that a woman of great importance conveys with her from her people's house is often implied as "Streedhan" and on a basic level is the property of the young woman, yet really generally viewed as their authentic due by the young men family. The complete to be paid as offer has no set norm, the gauge staggeringly depends upon the young men calling/social standing and is much of the time seen as the prep's family as the compensation they have made to train their child. The settlement system spread unabated to upsetting degrees taking cost of various energetic women. Because of the frankensteinian approach of the overall population the country saw the advancement of the shades of perniciousness of this system in a more extreme and genuine shape. The greater portion of the country mentioning and expecting the companion cost is stylish. Outrageous totals and other huge examinations are mentioned. Absurd late years and years the country has seen the wrongs of blessing structure fit as a fiddle.

KEYWORDS- Dowry Death, law, Indian Penal code, Legitimate security

## INTRODUCTION

In a more simple perspective, one may portray this custom as the unchallenged believed that the young woman's family is below average in leftover with the child's family, notwithstanding what her attributes are. Thusly they ought to be on their best lead also, offer rich "gifts" to fulfill the child's family. This ideal is so permeated in the brain of a significant number of Indians, they either in every practical sense, obliterate themselves financially remembering the ultimate objective to pay at the appropriate expense of the picked prep, or on the other hand make a proposal to slaughter the chance of this money related load by explicit sex un even untimely birth or female child murder. This manipulative system that has turned the custom of giving blessings and well wishes into a compulsory premium for money, respect and oppression, is the one of the major contributing parts ruining the advancement of the Indian culture where being a woman is as yet seen equivalent to being a weight. Social associations are made in heaven, is an adage. A woman of great importance leaves the parental home for the conjugal home, deserting sweet memories there with an assumption that she will see a different universe stacked with warmth in the home. She abandons her memories, just as her last name, Gotra and womanhood. She expects that not solely will be a young lady in law yet a young lady in all honesty. Goodness! The upsetting rising in the amount of the cases counting bullying to as of late wed young women for settlement crushes the fantasies. In laws are depicted to be out-laws for executing a manipulation through scare tactics which obliterates conjugal home. It has been penetrated practically all through the country and almost by all fragments of the overall population. The wealthy people with their accounted and unaccounted wealth have appreciated this everyday practice concerning ~Jiving and taking of settlement. They play out the social associations with remarkable service and show. The giving and taking of gift has been considered as a picture of high friendly magnificence and rank. The despicable effect of this preparation have pervaded the not-wealthy people of the overall population as indeed, even the people who experience share and associated offenses even passing at the tip might be a consuming issue of the Indian society since years. it's expanding step by step as a result of social legacy, antiquated attitude what's more, life vogue inside the family. endowment passing might be an enormous test to the stylish society, moral qualities, police, and expository experts further on lawful officials and equity not exclusively to dispose of this social peril anyway additionally to punish the guilty parties in successful way to structure the globe liberated from it for eternity. In greater part instances of lady slaughtering or lady of the hour consuming or settlement passing, disadvantage is framed by the actual female against their own sex. it's been now and again found that approach of mother by marriage is entirely unexpected from lady of the hour's mom. At first at the hour of wedding, money is given by lady's family according to request of the parents in law anyway by and by appetite of endowment is expanding phenomenally high that is trailed by torment of lady of the hour lastly winds up in her demise. In various words, in lady of the hour consuming cases, wrongdoing is regularly abetted and surprisingly carried out by the actual females. The unnatural demise of new wedded young lady in view of endowment is normal title text of every paper and media even these days. Self consuming by females when demise of her better half in Hindu local area is generally acknowledged and matter of pleased as in ' Pratha' or 'Joher'. be that as it may today, sizable measure of new wedded young ladies' square measure consumed alive by their spouses and/ or parents in law or constrained by them to complete their miserable life, several others square measure slaughtered starting so consumed to cover the wrongdoing. In dominant part of those cases, share is that the excellent intention behind this awful wrongdoing. Assurance of youthful wedded ladies badgering and cold-bloodedness because of endowment is duty of state. structure and media may likewise successfully contribute by creating mindfulness identifying with this issue and activating the help of society against this dread. we keep an eye on a necessity to battle along to complete this social wrongdoing always to get new cheerful skyline lifetime of wedded women.

## OBJECTIVES

The primary point of this exploration paper is to comprehend the idea of endowment passing and for recommending measures for its annulment totally in India and what are the causes causing it and for alluding the endowment passing related projects and enactments and to see whether it meets the closures of the equity.

## [61]DOWRY DEATH RELATED LAWS

The Indian Penal Code (I.P.C.), Criminal Procedure Code (Cr.P.C.) and Indian Evidence Act (I.E.A.) under the criminal law (Second Amendment) Act, 1983 and by President of India to deal with dowry death cases and of cruelty caused to married women. IPC SECTION 304-B At the point when the passing of a wedded lady is caused by any consumes or substantial damage or happens under irregular or suspicious conditions inside seven years of her marriage span and it is obviously appeared that soon before her demise she was subjected to cold-bloodedness or badgering or torment by her better half or any relative of her spouse or in laws for, or in association with, any interest for settlement, such passing should be called as "settlement passing", and such spouse or relative or in law s esteemed to have caused her demise. Whoever confers endowment passing might be rebuffed with detainment for a term least of seven years which may reach out to detainment forever.

IPC SECTION 498-A[62] This section speaks about cruelty caused to women by husband or relative of the husband. Whoever being the spouse or the relative of the spouse or in law of a lady, subjects such lady to cold-bloodedness or provocation or torment might be rebuffed with detainment for a term which may reach out up to three years and to pay fine.

61. https://acadpubl.eu/hub/2018-120-5/2/159.pdf
62. Pragnesh parmar dowry death and law –indian scenario published on 2nd October 2014

The mercilessness can be either mental or then again physical torment which drives the ladies to confer suicide or to cause genuine damage, or on the other hand threat to life or wellbeing.

IEA SECTION 113-A This section deals with presumption of abetment of suicide of a married women[63]. At the point when the inquiry is whether the commission of suicide by lady had been abetted by her better half or any relativ her better half and it is demonstrated that she had conferred suicide inside a time of seven a long time from the date of her oversee and her spouse or such relative of her better half had subjected to remorselessness, the court may assume, having respect to the various conditions of the case, that such suicide had been abetted by her better half or by such relative of her better half.

IEA SECTION 113-B This section deals with presumption of dowry death. At the point when the inquiry is whether a man has conferred the share passing of a lady and it is demonstrated that soon before her demise, such lady had been subjected by such individual to remorselessness or provocation for, or in association with, any interest for endowment, the court might assume that such individual had caused the share passing.

## ROLE OF FORENSIC EXPERT IN DOWRY DEATH

Logical experts come into picture so to speak right when blessing passing cases are shipped off them for after death assessment for getting imperative speculations. In expert's view, gift passing cases look like some other unnatural female passing cases yet. Strong obligation to the supported code for the conductance of after death in blessing downfall cases should be watched. Attempt to find out the explanation, thought of death and time since death and other huge real factors from the medico-genuine viewpoint to help value. Proximity of a lady expert in the assessment bunch is must to picture and examine all edges

---

63. Latha.k.s's dowry death implications of law published on January 1998

yet each case is amazing. An enormous part of the setbacks are young hitched women who are for the most part set apart as circumstantial passings, yet actually these are unquestionably not incidental cases yet are of deadly in nature. So it is the fundamental commitment of legitimate experts to look for the right justification demise dependent on critical data and characteristic standards in sensible manner and approach.

## SOCIAL FACTORS OF DOWRY DEATH

Offer is a social sin, which is typical among upper and middle class classes of Hindu gathering of India, and is the key factor forunnatural passings in as of late married females since years. Other than share, obliviousness, coordinated or love social associations, kid social associations, joint family structure, oedipal incredibleness of relative, joblessness and monetary dependence of life partners on their people, close whole dependence of women or their significant other or potentially parents in law, inebriation, callousness and faithlessness of the companions and need of government backed retirement among Hindu women are other contributory components impacting the intimate bliss in one or various ways. Offer has quite recently a solitary finish of the shore of social maltreatment sea; inside a comparative field are inhumanity, discipline, and assault, physical or mental torture thus forward. After marriage, young woman is drive into a dark world what's more, is gotten into arrangement of vulnerabilities what's more, subsequently she is totally on the altruism of the life partner or possibly his family members who may or will not really like her.

## [64]MEDICAL AND LEGAL ASPECTS OF DOWRY DEATH

A portion of the essential medico which warrant see have been managed in here to thoroughly consider the fragile

---

64.  https://acadpubl.eu/hub/2018-120-5/2/159.pdf

circumstances looked by legal specialists in their schedule hone. The essential viewpoint is that not just the police should act instantly to maintain a strategic distance from destruction of basic pieces of information at the scene of wrongdoing yet additionally police should act instantly in enlisting all such gripes immediately. In the event that an uncommon team/cell are kept up at that point this ought to likewise be educated for examinations of each case. Besides, if neighbourhood police is lingering behind or demonstrating a deferring arrangement then either the predominant officers are drawn nearer or intentional associations be drawn nearer for the best possible examination to be finished. Inclusion of media additionally centers a solid mindfulness about the event of wrongdoing. In the event that the casualty is alive after the occurrence at that point incite endeavors ought to be made to record a assertion by a skillful specialist. Passing on assertion has lawful authenticity as the Indian law assumes that a man who acknowledges that her leaving is behind and coming will come clean with just and never lies. Regardless, from our perspective, in specific conditions female losses who make kicking the can insistence, may give fake information, particularly if the lady is proceed with tortured for a significant long time together or, more than likely is truly debilitate or influenced by drug or needs to get the inevitable destiny of her young people.

## LEGAL PROTECTION OF WOMEN IN INDIA

The rule of sexual orientation balance is cherished in the Indian Constitution in its Preamble, Key Rights, Fundamental Duties and Directive Principles. The Constitution not just awards correspondence to ladies, yet additionally enables the State to embrace proportions of positive separation for ladies. Inside the system of a vote based commonwealth, our laws, improvement approaches, Plans and projects have focused on ladies' headway in various circles. India has likewise endorsed different global shows and basic freedoms instruments resolving to get equivalent privileges of ladies. Key among them is the confirmation of the Convention on Elimination of All Forms of Discrimination against Women (CEDAW) in 1993. "Endorsing CEDAW stays among the incomplete business of the Civil Rights development."

## POWERFUL STRIDES TO BE TAKEN

Boycott of giving and taking settlement Prohibition Act, 1961, is that the one that is most commonly tested since its initiation wherever the country. there's no conflict that there's partner degree truly expanding wrongdoing against women's hands of their spouses and/or in laws. To impact this part 304 and 498 - A (Cruelty by spouse or in were consolidated inside the Indian board code inside the center 1980's. A re-assessment of endowment Denial Act, 1961 should be done again on the grounds that the law has really didn't the executives the wrongdoings against women's or in outcome didn't fabricate the significant results. In addition, the endowment Prohibition Act, 1961 being a authoritative demonstration, here and there police don't make strides or take a parcel of consideration in it, a great deal of value because of offenses underneath the demonstration square measure treated as understandable offenses without a doubt confined capacities. Serious punishment is to shelter those that take endowment and cruel laws be outlined for share associated provocation and endowment passings. Exacting laws should to try and be instituted to preclude remarriages for such men UN organizations spouses are scorched alive and/or the young men who are fixed in endowment passings until the release of extreme judgment. Plus, an exceptional team of police should be instilled ex this reason, and quick police examinations should be finished. endless recognition is furthermore a prerequisite for all enrolled settlement passing cases each at locale and state high court level all together that equity should be conveyed at the soonest.

# JUSTIFICATION OF DOWRY DEATH WHY DOES IT OCCUR?

For what reason do settlement passings happen? This was the principle issue of stress of a sociological report by Nalini Singh considering an audit of the social associations of 38 youngsters, developed 17-24 a long time, in all of which the life partner passed on an unnatural destruction, apparently in light of the fact that of harassing over settlement. She suggested that it is chiefly the cultural perspective on woman being less useful than man that portray woman's position in the public field. This shows in what she calls "Zero-political Status", and refusal of fundamental social correspondence to them. She watches that blessing is an undeniable statement of the way that one's sexual direction chooses one's worth or criticalness. Since worth is appropriated inconsistent among the sexual orientations during labor, worth-need among females can be adjusted by material added substances that is share. The establishments of this worth absence of women are so significant set up that even the women who secure more than their companions are caused to feel a obligation to supply settlement product and ventures along after their marriage likewise actually like the women who win nothing. The gift, thusly, she watches, don't occur considering the way that there is a confound between endowments mentioned by parents in law and presents got, yet since young married women ordinarily have no political criticalness in their new families. The persevering interest for enrichment is yet one of the habits by which the insufficient political status is abused. This need is used to mishandle her in perpetual various manners also. Thus, she says, the term 'settlement is a misnomer since share related baiting occurs as a part of a greater order to abuse a human with zero-political status. Offer is hardly ever the single justification affirmed settlement. As such, whether or not solicitations for settlement were to be satisfied totally, youthful women would continue confronting torture and baiting in their parents in law homes because of their solely approved deficiency that keeps them from getting their fundamental basic freedoms. As shown by Nalini Singh, from the most timely days of a marriage the parents in law obliterate the existence of a woman of great importance on the assumption that the youngster has given up her total being to them; she turns around in opposite to show that she has no political status, furthermore, sneaks through the base of the master structure; while her people guarantee her that implosion is decent in woman.

## CONCLUSION

Dowry Death is a burning-through regular issue of the Indian culture. It should be recognized that required result can't be gotten by authorizing of law alone against share. This social criticize should be attacked by a multipronged and formed methodology by police, women government assistance affiliations, assumed open laborers, and lawful and by giving block control to every single liable gathering. Regardless, a change enlightening status of the females and giving less requesting openings for work at the entrance step or autonomous work workplaces will assist with binding the events of offer Likewise, informative cum care projects should be made agreeable break of marriage to stop the mate from eating up blenders, drugs or then again wagering, keeping to monogamy what's more, acquiring money earnestly by sheer steady work as opposed to making want for money sans work. Through our eyes, a rational and conventional methodology on the recently referenced issue will totally be helpful. Repayment is paid as cash and items, for instance, embellishments, nuclear family mechanical assemblies and automobiles to the spouse or his people by the woman's family. It has been illegal in India since 1961 yet remains common – with dreadful outcomes. Women have submitted self destruction since they couldn't stand up to goading over enrichment portion. Others have been executed by their life partner or parents in law for not dealing with their settlement demands. Around 8,000 settlement are recorded each year in India, as shown by the public bad behaviors bits of knowledge office. Two women in their 20s submitted self destruction over gift goading around a similar time a month prior in Gurgaon, a cutting edge satellite city of Delhi, where the amount of settlement climbed from 12 of each 2015 to 20 per year prior, according to the Times of India, a development of 66.7 for every penny. For another circumstance point by point a month prior in Hyderabad, a 21-year-old woman kicked the container after her better half and watchmen in-law poured light fuel on her and put a match to her considering an contention about settlement. 18On Monday, an item work in Hyderabad was represented to have balanced herself in the wake of being bothered for settlement portions by her significant other, indeed, even in spite of the way that her family had authoritatively given him show up and liberal proportions of gold and cash at the period of marriage. There is no huge reduction in marital crime percentages even after the enactment of settlement preclusion laws in India. Hence speculation is demonstrated.

## REFERENCES

1.  Vij K. Textbook of Forensic Medicine and Toxicology. 5th edition. Elsevier, 2011, 206.

2.  Reddy KSN. The Essentials of Forensic Medicine and Toxicology. 31st edition. Om Sai Graphics, 2012, 273.

3.  Mathiharan K, Patnaik AK. (edi.) Modi's Medical Jurisprudence and Toxicology. 23rd edition. LexisNexis, Butterworths, 2006, 21.

4.  Parikh CK. Parikh's Textbook of Medical Jurisprudence and Toxicology, 5th edition. 1996, 385- 386.

5.  Bardale R. Principles of Forensic Medicine and Toxicology. 1 Jaypee Brothers Medical Publishers, 2011, 272.

6.  Das Gupta et al. Burn wife syndrome. Ann. Acad. Med. Singapore, 1984; 13(I):37-42.

7.  Satpathy DK. Burning Brides medico-legal study. Med. 14:547-552.

8.  Bhullar DS et al. Profile of unnatural female deaths (between 18 of age) in Govt. Medical College/ Rajindra Hospital, Patiala (India). Journal of Forensic Medicine and Toxicology. 1996; 13(3-4):5.

9.  Rao NKG. Study of in Manipur. Journal of Forensic Medicine and Toxicology. 1997; 14(2):57-59.

10. Parmar P, Saiyed ZG, Patel P. Study of pattern of head injury in drivers of two wheeler auto vehicle accidents. Indian Journal of Forensic Medicine and Toxicology. 2012; 6(2):248-252.

11. Singh JP. Dowry in India: A search for new Social identity, The Eastern Anthropologist. 2005; 58(2)199- 220.

12. Negi CF, Saravanan S. Violence against women in India: A literature review, Instt. For Social Studies Trust, 2000.

13. Singh M. Dowry as a factor of violence in Marriage: A study of Women seeking help in Family Counseling Centers in Chandigarh. International Journal of Advancements in Research and Technology, 2013; 2(6).

14. Paul MC. Dowry and position of women in India: A study of Delhi Metropolis, New Delhi: Inter-India Publications, 1986; (9).

# 9

# GENDER INEQUALITY IN HINDU AND MUSLIM PERSONAL LAWS IN INDIA

## ABSTRACT

The paper expects to feature the situation with ladies in Hindu and Muslim strict individual laws and giving the brief looks at the impacts of such close to home laws on the existences of ladies. To accomplish the target of the paper, broad exploration has been done and the examination has been so written down. Regardless, starting point of the idea of strict individual laws and their particular change by the State has been covered and appropriately portrayed. Current status of ladies in Hindu and Muslim strict individual laws are shown which incorporates how the state of strict individual laws has repercussions for the plan and extent of different laws. Impacts of such laws on the existences of ladies of each layer of the general public are covered. This paper further advances and investigations the current circumstance of individual laws regarding ladies in India and the equivalent have been examined in the light of existing rules and case laws. Milestone decisions have been utilized to additionally comprehend the legal part of the laws predominant in the general public. Difficulties like why this uniqueness actually exists and what impacts it will have on the people in the future are fundamentally examined. A contention for a reconceptualization of classifications that take into consideration seeking after contrasts and equity together is created. In spite of the fact that the Indian constitution endowments ladies indistinguishable rights and prospects, and an amount of liberal laws, for example, the Equal Remuneration Act declare this worth, India's legitimate course of action keeps on separating counter to ladies. This is generally evident in two regions: the legacy laws, and separation and upkeep laws. Public exposition on eliminating legitimate insight against females has focused on the case for a uniform common code. This case has generally speaking been kept up by Hindu strict leaders and strongly went against by Muslim and Christian strict leaders. In fact, in any case, essentially all close to home laws, be it Hindu, Muslim, or Parsi, separate against ladies. In thought ladies are intrinsically guaranteed the rudimentary right to property. In work out, the liberal nature of the constitution is repaid by a comparative arrangement of individual law that limits women's legacy, security, and upkeep rights. Legacy laws are a striking case of sex foul play in the control and course of properties.

## [65]INTRODUCTION

Contemporary India is a multicultural society that is pluralistic regarding strict law. As there are various religions so there are countless individual laws too which supervises everybody of different religions. The term 'individual laws' incorporates the scriptural orders and standard acts of that specific religion. Strict individual laws insinuate the guidelines managing the course of action of marriage and its crumbling; the different rights, responsibilities and cutoff points of marriage; the association among watchmen furthermore, youngsters; intimate property; kid authority or guardianship; and legacy. These laws relate stories about the lifestyle, practices, feelings and characteristics that help to shape our points of view about which we are, the spot we started from, and where we are going. Every religion has its own personal laws, for example, Hindus, Muslims, Parsis,

---

65. Bina Agarwal, Redefining Family Law in India, 306-354, (Routledge Delhi, 2007)

Jains, Christians, etc. There is no uniform common code in India. The ladies have less rights than the men under the strict individual laws. The strict individual laws bring forward various restrictions; for instance man driven society, early marriage, blessing, forceful conduct at home, etc. The overall population has plonked choices on the ladies. The situation with ladies is of unimaginable concern as these laws portray ladies in subordinate situation to men. As a thought, "sexual orientation disparity" implies the obvious or covered contrasts among individuals considering the execution of the sexual direction. The term 'sex' outlines the social and social idea about everybody. Sexual orientation did not depend on the organic attributes. Sociologists portray sex dissimilarity as the differentiation in the status, force and prominence ladies and men have in gatherings, collectivities and social orders. Ladies need to experience with an enormous number of irregularities which brief such immense quantities of obstructions in their journey. The women feel unacceptable just as vulnerable considering the way that the youth of the youthful women has been done as such as to not speak more loudly against such partitions. In spite of the way that the council has endeavored the undertakings to lift the situation with ladies, yet there is need to change the considering design individuals to give feeling of belief to ladies about their latent capacity.

## HINDU LAW

Females' property rights in the Male-controlled Family. A Hindu father in male-controlled family revered total force like the Roman father in ancient Rome. The sacred texts unquestionably sponsored a lot to stamp the father, the holder of the family a flat out ruler. Manu said that three people, a spouse, a child and a slave are pronounced by law to have overall no abundance only their own; the abundance which they may procure is routinely gained for the man to whom they have a place. Essentially Narada had faith in the view that a child could be autonomous just if his folks are dead; during their lifetime he is needy despite the fact that he is developed old. So in a male-controlled family females and posterity didn't have property rights. The spouse was put into the arrangement of assets and slaves. They had an troubled and curbed life in the old male-controlled families.

## WIDOW'S DOMAIN

A Hindu Joint family contains people. The married and unmarried girls stayed as offshoots of the joint family. The male partners are coparceners with right of survivorship. The techniques for survivorship had been set by Narada. He said that if among a few individuals, one childless passes on or turns into a strict parsimonious, the other will partition property aside from stridhanam. So widows are banned from survivorship. Anyway this old guideline has been canceled by the Women's Right to Property Act 1937. According to the Act the solaces of male coparceners delegate on their expiry upon widows. This organized Hindu women's space.

## GENDER JUSTICE: TRANSFORMATIONS IN HINDU LAW

The times past of Hindu Law change accompanies the Hindu Law advisory group (Rau Board of trustees) shaped in 1941. It was followed by another Committee in 1944. The council finally presented its report to the Federal Parliament in 1947. The recognitions of the council were questioned in the common Parliament. There was intense resistance in spite of the establishment of monogamy, separate, destruction of coparcenary and legacy to little girls from the ordinary Hindu public. The Congress delegate from West Bengal battled that as it were ladies of the lavender, lipstick and vanity sack assortment were keen on the Bill[66]. There were additionally stresses among the ordinary Hindu men that if females were accepted property

---

66. Paras Diwan, "Daughters Right to Inheritance and Fragmentation of Holdings" SC (J) 15. (1978)

rights relations would fall. In 1948 there stood an All India Anti-Hindu Code Show. [67]It was asserted that the organization of women's part would prompt the breakdown of Hindu family framework which had been involved as a co-employable framework for endless time periods for protection of family bonds and resources. It was likewise called attention to that the incorporation of girl in the line of legacy is because of European impact. Despite the fact that the upper male congress leaders were against the Bill, Jawaharlal Nehru and Dr. Ambedkar were devoted to the Bill. Nehru exclusively put stock in ladies' declarations to comparable property rights. Dr. Ambedkar needed to battle impressively because of the vigorous resistance from the fortification of higher class Hindus.

## THE ORIGIN OF THE CONCEPT OF RELIGIOUS PERSONAL LAWS

India's general set of laws is affected by customary law framework – a relic of British imperialism. In the midst of colonization, the standard normal association between a legal system and its overall population was viciously upset doubly by this assessment. Indians came to have a genuine structure made considering the necessities of an inside and out various society, that of England. Nevertheless, while laws in England have given up or changed most of these authentic thoughts, India keeps up the "show" of the pioneer laws. The thought of strict individual laws is one of those thoughts. Step by step authoritative changes were additionally presented, yet notwithstanding these progressions that the strict individual laws are changeless actually endures. The act of applying laws of strict networks in close to home matters was viewed as the "saving" of strict laws, to some extent as a result of the language utilized. Incredibly, English approaches figured out what ought to be assigned as an individual matter. One checked component of most strict individual laws is that ladies have less rights than men. The state has explicitly used the

---

67. Ibid

dispute of strict holiness of these laws anyway at various events introduced legitimate changes. By far most of the movements have been introduced in the Hindu Laws anyway the changes in the minority organizations' laws have been all the seriously halting. For example, in 2005, in the Hindu Succession Act, it was proposed remembering the ultimate objective to make girls compare coparceners; in any case, the authorization by the by still leaves ladies with lesser rights than men. It is in these particular conditions that sexual orientation disparity for Indian ladies will likely be refined by introducing an organization of basic family law that would prompt see the standard of sexual orientation equity as the describing feature of the law.

## WOMEN IN MUSLIM LAW

Islam implies tranquility, and acquiescence. As per Agnes, Islam likewise implies harmony and accommodation. "Shariah is an Arabic word that implies the "Way to be followed," alluding to various legitimate directives known as Islamic law. The essential wellspring of Islamic law is the Quran, which Muslims accept to be God's words. Despite the fact that the Quran contains legitimate remedies, it is principally worried about broad moral standards and rules as opposed to severe guidelines. Along these lines, the Quran is enhanced by different sources to frame the premise of Sharia. The Shariah is a consequence of what individuals comprehended out of those blessed proclamations. The cardinal thought is unique in relation to what we got the type of Shariah. Ladies are myrmidon to men in this man centric culture.

## LEGACY RIGHTS OF MUSLIM WOMEN UNDER THE MUSLIM PERSONAL LAW

Muslim ladies rights have been an issue of discussion ever from when the Constitution appeared in 1950. Muslim law (Shariah) is pondered by numerous individuals as male-controlled furthermore, tyrannical to ladies. Anyway the Quran has discussed women's concerns fourteen hundred years back by producing a few changes to improve the situation of ladies in spite of the fact that these changes don't seem, by all accounts, to be embraced practically speaking in Muslim society these days. In spite of the fact that Islam as demonstrated to the prophet Mohammed isn't tyrannical to ladies its adaptation administered in the family law, and day by day living is male-controlled.by Shariat.

## PROPERTY RIGHTS OF MUSLIM WOMEN

The Muslim Jurists gave impressive significance to the laws of legacy and they were absolutely not burnt out on retelling the adage of the prophet. The Prophet accepted that assimilate the laws of legacy and bestow it in the people for they are one-portion of significant data and current authors have regarded the framework for its adequacy and endorsed merit. Macnaghten verbalizes that in these laws we find abundant consideration paid to the interests of each one of those whom nature places in the primary position of our kind gestures and for sure it is hard to consider any framework containing rules all the more carefully and evenhanded. The Islamic law of treasure contains two separate basics, the custom of soonest Arabia and headings set by Quran and the Ancestor of Islam. The Koranic change came as a system upon the early ancestral law.

A considerable lot of the pervasive, cultural and monetary dissimilarities were adapted to that reason Koran might be signified as an amending Act.

## PROPERTY RIGHTS OF MUSLIM WOMEN UNDER THE CUSTOMARY LAW

In pre-Islamic Arabia the law of treasure was grounded on comradeship-in arms and from this time forward indeed, even spouse and kids were forgotten about from heritage. In datum the law of legacy was based on the estimations of agnatic preferring and notwithstanding of females. Consequently a girl or a sister or daughter's child or sister's child couldn't prevail to the property.t is clear from this that prior to the appearance of Islam females were seized of their entitlement to heritage as well as their very destiny was in the impact of her husband's band or with her family members. In the pre-Islamic culture guys savored better hand over ladies in issues related than heritage. At the point when a man lost his life, his replacement would attest the directly absurd and marries her. Consequently after marriage, he dismisses her entitlement to declare the piece of heritage organized by the settlement. He can likewise take the wedding blessing and solicitation another man to wed her. Moreover, illegitimate kids unquestionably not got; rather they were abused and not saw after well and little youngsters would transform into casualties of sexual maltreatment.

## CONCLUSION

The Hindu Succession Act of 1956 was imagined to extend the privileges of Hindu ladies. In spite of the fact that the Act has consolidated some sexual orientation abberations, many till now proceed. Under Hindu law, children have a self-ruling offer in the family property. Notwithstanding, daughters☐ parcels are grounded on the offer got by their dad. Consequently, a dad can proficiently repudiate a little girl by giving up a lot of the family property, however the child will stay to have a segment in his individual right. Also, wedded little girls, even those fronting conjugal aggravation, have no homegrown rights in the family home. Despite the fact that laws themselves have not been sex evenhanded, even the feeble guidelines ensuring females have not been adequately applied. Thusly, in practice females keep on having close to nothing access to land and property, a central wellspring of income and proceeding with monetary wellbeing. Indeed at the point when the state ponders rights on the oppressed via land change, the proprietorship to the land is reliably in the assignment of the male head and is not really held along with his life partner. Also, legitimate rancher entryways in north India have lately needed to deny females of insignificant property rights. Lot of females keep on being neglectful of their privileges of legacy; and, where educated, social forces keep ladies from testing these rights. Females themselves habitually repulse varieties in legacy plans, with two of three females being evidently against young ladies getting an equivalent segment with young men in parental things.

By standard definition, the family properties are those resources accomplished from father or fatherly granddad or fatherly incredible granddad or segment accomplished on parcel or self-achieved properties or particular properties of an individual tossed into the joined family properties. In the Indian Succession Act, 1925, which is additionally relevant to Hindus, the two people have unhindered right of testamentary character, while the Muslim Law limits the said right to just 1/third of the space subsequent to lessening burial service consumptions and unpaid debts. The Law Commission has been trusted with the obligation of auditing the Central Acts to smooth out them and to take out abnormalities, ambiguity and separation. From July 2005 the new Act has come into power and the girl is allotted a similar part as is assigned to a child. The little girl will reserve a privilege to state parcel in the joint family properties notwithstanding the option to declare right of segment in the home place of the joint family and she will likewise have an option to declare segment during the life expectancy of her dad. This chance is simply given to Hindu females. The laws relevant to Muslims and Christians don't give comparable situation to females.

At the point when the constitution of India and the laws as of late authorized are in endorsement of giving equivalent position to the females, the females are worried in requesting lesser than what they are qualified for and they are attempting to apply the Women's Bill where they will have just 33% right.

Both Hindu and Muslim individual laws don't perceive conjugal property. Henceforth, at the time of separate, females reserve no options to their family or to different resources assembled during marriage; in outcome, their aids to the upkeep of the family and social event of family resources go unseen and unrewarded. To cite from Justice Sujata V. Manohar of Supreme Court of India "It is difficult to kill profound situated social qualities or to modify customs that sustain segregation. It is popular to criticize the job of law change in achieving social change. Clearly law, without help from anyone else, may not be sufficient. Law is just an instrument. It should be adequately utilized. Furthermore, this successful use depends as much on a strong legal executive as on the social will to change. A functioning social change development, whenever joined by legitimate change, appropriately upheld, can change society."

## BIBLIOGRAPHY

1.  A. Bindra, Women and Human Rights. Manglam Publishers and Distributors, Delhi, 2007, 31.

2.  Alka Singh, Women in Muslim Personal Law. Rawat Publications, 1992.

3.  Anthony Giddens, Sociology. Polity Press, UK, 2006, 468.

4.  Flavia Agnes, Constitutional Challenges, Communal Hues and Reforms within Personal Laws. Combat Law. 2004.

5.  Gopal G., Gender and Economic Inequality in India: The Legal Connection. Boston College Third World Law Journal, 1993.

6.  Kulwant Gill, Hindu Women's Right to Property in India. Deep & Deep Publications Pvt. Ltd., New Delhi, 1986.

7.  M. Chawla, Gender Justice: Women and Law in India. Deep and Deep Publications, New Delhi, 2006.

8. P. K. Das, Handbook on Hindu Succession (Property Rights of Women and Daughters). Universal Law Publishing Co. Pvt. Ltd., Delhi, 2007.

9. R. K. Sinha, Women Across Generation. Mohit Publications, New Delhi, 2010.

10. R. Mukherjee, Women, Law and Free Legal Aid in India. Deep and Deep Publications, New Delhi, 1998.

11. S. A. Kader, Muslim Law of Marriage and Succession in India. Easter Law House, New Delhi, 1998.

12. S. M. Asay, J. Defrain, M. Metzger & B. Moyer (Eds.). Family Violence from the Global Perspective Sage Publication, 2014, 69.

## WEBSITES

1. www.heinonline.org

2. www.jstor.org

3. www.manupatrafast.com

4. www.scconline.com

# 10

# GOOD BYE PATRIARCHY

## ABSTRACT

Man controlled society can be characterized as a social framework in what men hold essential power and rule in jobs of political administration, moral position, social advantage, and control of property. This obsolete arrangement of social association has decided and molded the existences of ladies and young ladies since hundreds of years, and keeps on doing as such. Ladies are given a role as more vulnerable creatures needing assurance; compliant, and less significant than men, and are denied the rights, openings, decisions and pay that are offered to men. These difficulties are substantially more articulated and noticeable for young ladies having a place with non-industrial nations and low-pay families, where the disparities of pay and sexual orientation are woven together in an unpredictable web that further denies ladies the fundamental right to balance. While numerous nations across the globe have started gaining ground towards obliterating man controlled society and setting up uniformity, it is far-fetched that any of us will see sexual orientation equality in the course of our lives, the Global Gender Gap Report 2020 uncovers that sex equality won't be achieved for 99.5 years.

Keywords- Society, Cultural value, Moral and Ethics.

# PUBLIC POLICY FOR THE EMPOWERMENT OF WOMEN (2001)

The guideline of sexual orientation correspondence is revered in the Indian Constitution in its Preamble, Fundamental Rights, Fundamental Duties and Directive Principles. The Constitution awards uniformity to ladies, yet in addition engages the State to embrace proportions of positive segregation for ladies. Inside the structure of a vote based country, our laws, improvement strategies, Plans and projects have focused on ladies' headway in various circles. From the Fifth Five Year Plan (1974-78) onwards has been a stamped move in the way to deal with ladies' issues from government assistance to advancement. Lately, the strengthening of ladies has been perceived as the focal issue in deciding the situation with ladies. The National Commission for Women was set up by an Act of Parliament in 1990 to defend the rights and legitimate qualifications of ladies. The 73rd and 74th Amendments (1993) to the Constitution of India have given to reservation of seats in the neighborhood assemblages of Panchayats and Municipalities for ladies, establishing a solid framework for their interest in dynamic at the nearby levels.

India has additionally endorsed different worldwide shows and common liberties instruments resolving to get equivalent privileges of ladies. Key among them is the sanction of the Convention on Elimination of All Forms of Discrimination Against Women (CEDAW) in 1993.

The Mexico Plan of Action (1975), the Nairobi Forward Looking Strategies (1985), the Beijing Declaration just as the Platform for Action (1995) and the Outcome Document embraced by the UNGA Session on Gender Equality and Development and Peace for the 21st century, named "Further activities and activities to carry out the Beijing Declaration and the Platform for Action" have been wholeheartedly supported by India for suitable development.

The Policy additionally observes the responsibilities of the Ninth Five Year Plan and the other Sectoral Policies identifying with strengthening of Women.

The ladies' development and a wide-spread organization of non-Government Organizations which have solid grass-roots presence and profound knowledge into ladies' interests have contributed in moving activities for the strengthening of ladies.

However, there still exists a wide hole between the objectives articulated in the Constitution, enactment, strategies, plans, programs, and related components from one perspective and the situational truth of the situation with ladies in India, on the other. This has been broke down broadly in the Report of the Committee on the Status of Women in India, "Towards Equality", 1974 and featured in the National Perspective Plan for Women, 1988-2000, the Shramshakti Report, 1988 and the Platform for Action, Five Years After-An appraisal"

Gender difference shows itself in different structures, the most clear being the pattern of ceaselessly declining female proportion in the populace over the most recent couple of many years. Social generalizing and savagery at the homegrown and cultural levels are a portion of different appearances. Victimization young lady kids, juvenile young ladies and ladies perseveres in pieces of the country.

The fundamental reasons for sex disparity are identified with social and monetary construction, which depends on casual and formal standards, and practices.

Consequently, the entrance of ladies especially those having a place with more fragile segments including Scheduled Castes/Scheduled Tribes/Other in reverse Classes and minorities, dominant part of whom are in the provincial regions and in the casual, disorderly area – to schooling, wellbeing and gainful assets, among others, is insufficient. Consequently, they remain to a great extent minimized, poor and socially prohibited.

## OBJECTIVE AND OBJECTIVES [68]

The objective of this Policy is to achieve the headway, improvement and strengthening of ladies. The Policy will be generally scattered in order to empower dynamic cooperation of all partners for accomplishing its objectives. In particular, the targets of this Policy incorporate

i. Creating a climate through sure monetary and social strategies for full advancement of ladies to empower them to understand their maximum capacity

ii. The by law and accepted delight in every basic liberty and key opportunity by ladies on equivalent premise with men taking all things together circles – political, monetary, social, social and common

iii. Equal admittance to investment and dynamic of ladies in friendly, political and monetary existence of the country

iv. Equal admittance to ladies to medical services, quality schooling at all levels, profession and professional direction, business, equivalent compensation, word related wellbeing and wellbeing, government backed retirement and public office and so on

v. Strengthening overall sets of laws focused on end of all types of victimization ladies

vi. Changing cultural mentalities and local area rehearses by dynamic cooperation and inclusion of the two people.

vii. Mainstreaming a sex point of view in the improvement interaction.

---

68. https://wcd.nic.in/womendevelopment/national-policy-women-empowerment

viii. Elimination of separation and all types of savagery against ladies and the young lady kid; and

ix. Building and reinforcing associations with common society, especially ladies' associations.

## STATUS OF LADIES IN INDIA

Properly did Swami Vivekanand say, 'Similarly as a bird can not fly with one wing just, a Nation can not walk forward if the ladies are given up'. People are the two openings of an ideal entirety. Strength is a result of their association their partition brings about shortcoming. Each has what different doesn't have. Each finishes the other, and is finished by other. Etymologically, the word 'lady' mean - half of man. The connection of the male and female is very much delineated in our Nyaya Darshan by the similarity of brain and matter, which implies that man and lady are firmly connected with one another, as the spirit and body. Accordingly the ladies should be regarded.

## THE SOCIO-ECONOMIC STATUS OF WOMEN IN INDIA ANCIENT TO MODERN ERA

There is no uncertainty that we are amidst an incredible unrest throughout the entire existence of ladies. The proof is all over; the voice of ladies is progressively heard in Parliament, courts and in the roads. While ladies in the West needed to battle for longer than a century to get a portion of their essential rights, similar to one side to cast a ballot, the Constitution of India gave ladies equivalent rights with men all along. Lamentably, ladies in this nation are for the most part ignorant of their privileges in light of lack of education and the abusive custom. Names like Kalpana Chawla: The Indian conceived, who battled her way up into NASA and was the primary ladies in space, and Indira Gandhi: The Iron Woman of India was the Prime Minister of the Nation, Beauty Queens like Aishwarya Rai and Susmita Sen, and Mother Teresa are not agent of the state of Indian ladies.

# [69]VICIOUSNESS TOWARDS WOMAN

1. Segment 498A: of the Indian Penal Code (IPC), which characterizes the offense of marital brutality, was embedded into the IPC by a revision in 1983

2. Aggressive behavior at home in Marriage: The point of this article is to isolate this evil from the other honest standards, along these lines attempting to make a psychological barrier or obstruction among individuals towards the unnecessary brutality.

3. Aggressive behavior at home Act - Fundamental rights: Domestic brutality is unfortunately a reality in Indian culture, an axiom.

4. In the Indian Enslavement of ladies rights lead to infringement of common freedoms: Human rights as an issue possesses the focal point of the audience in contemporary public discussion

5. Eve prodding In India And Tortious Liabilities: The term Eve prodding is utilized to allude to inappropriate behavior of ladies out in the open spots

6. Lady of the hour consuming and Laws in India: The arrangement of endowment is profound established in the Indian culture since the beginning of the set of experiences

7. Law, Women and Advertisements: The Advertising Standards Council's Code for Self guideline characterizes an legitimate situation of Eunuchs: This article is an uncommon and touchy article which dives Ladies Suffrage. A similar viewpoint toward ladies' democratic right among Scandinavian and Middle Eastern nations - with a concentration in Iran

---

69. http://www.legalserviceindia.com/laws/women_issues.htm

8. Security of Women from Domestic Violence Act, 2005: Despite of these enactments there is no enactment which especially Individual Dignity. Dignity is an all inclusive human concern. Its ethical plan is to endeavor a twofold sort of assessment of the

9. Business Sex Workers: The business sex specialist has been an all inclusive being all through development as prostitution

10. Ladies and Violence: Violence influences the existences of millions of ladies around the world, taking all things together financial and instructive classes

11. Abusive behavior at home Act, 2005-A Bane Or A Boon?: Domestic viciousness is one of the gravest and the most unavoidable basic liberties infringement.A Woman Can't Rape Woman: In State Govt. V. Sheodayal (1956 Cr LJ 83 M.P) M.P High court thought that humility of a lady can be shocked by another ladies u/s 354.

12. Privileges of Second Wife: Second marriage, during the means of the primary marriage, is illicit

13. Savagery against ladies: This examination paper presents the conversation of legitimate reactions to brutality against ladies.

14. Savagery against lady - Issue of Honor executing: A lady can be focused by people inside her family for an assortment of reasons, including: declining to go into a masterminded marriage

15. Would women be able to be Karta?: The Karta of a Hindu joint Family in Hindu Law is the senior most individual from the family

16. Family law a total guide on family laws in India.

[70]Guaranteeing the rights of women and giving them opportunities to reach their full potential is critical not only for attaining gender equality, but also for meeting a wide range of international development goals. Empowered women and girls contribute to the health and productivity of their families, communities, and countries, creating a ripple effect that benefits everyone.

The word gender describes the socially-constructed roles and responsibilities that societies consider appropriate for men and women. Gender equality means that men and women have equal power and equal opportunities for financial independence, education, and personal development.

[71]In describing violence against women as a form of discrimination under Article 1 of the Convention on All Forms of Discrimination Against Women (GA Resolution 180/34), the CEDAW Committee made an important point about direct and indirect discrimination: it includes acts and situations which are created with the **purpose** of discriminating against women - that is, intentional discrimination which is done with the aim of discrimination - and acts and situations which have the **effect** of discriminating against women. **Gender pay gaps,** for example, may not have been planned to discriminate against women, or be intended to discriminate against women, but if the outcome is less favourable for women than for men, then this is a form of discrimination that the State is legally obliged to address. Article 1 of CEDAW (GA Resolution 34/180).

---

70. https://www.peacecorps.gov/educators/resources/global-issues-gender-equality-and-womens-empowerment  /

71. https://www.unodc.org/e4j/en/crime-prevention-criminal-justice/module-10/key-issues/2--human-rights-approaches-to-violence-against-women.html

## [72]INDIAN JUDICIAL LEGAL SYSTEMS

Legal-judicial system will be made more responsive and gender sensitive to women's needs, especially in cases of domestic violence and personal assault. New laws will be enacted and existing laws reviewed to ensure that justice is quick and the punishment meted out to the culprits is commensurate with the severity of the offence.

At the initiative of and with the full participation of all stakeholders including community and religious leaders, the Policy would aim to encourage changes in personal laws such as those related to marriage, divorce, maintenance and guardianship so as to eliminate discrimination against women.

The evolution of property rights in a patriarchal system has contributed to the subordinate status of women. The Policy would aim to encourage changes in laws relating to ownership of property and inheritance by evolving consensus in order to make them gender just.

## CONCLUSION

All in all, ladies can be amazing entertainers for harmony, security, and flourishing. At the point when they take an interest in harmony measures and other proper dynamic cycles, they can assume a significant part in starting and motivating advancement on common freedoms, equity, public compromise and financial renewal. It very well may be seen unmistakably from the above conversation that sexual orientation balance is very fundamental to accomplish the objective of ladies strengthening. It is seen that ladies in India have been exposed to different kinds of separation and handicaps towards delight in advantages of advancement ensuing upon debilitation. Thus the strengthening of ladies could be conceivable through fulfillment of sexual

---

72.  https://wcd.nic.in/womendevelopment/national-policy-women-empowerment

orientation balance. In request to advance sexual orientation correspondence in financial turn of events, the accompanying measures can be thought of.

## REFERENCES

1. Bradshaw, S., Castellino, J., and Diop, B. (2013, May 20). Women's role in economic development: Overcoming the constraints. Background Paper for the High-Level Panel of Eminent Persons on the Post-2015 Development 20 Paris, France and New York, USA:Sustainable Development Solutions Network. 2013. Available at http://unsdsn.org/resources

2. Castellino, J. (2013, January 15). Social inclusion and human rights: Implications for 2030 and beyond. Background Paper for the High-Level Panel of Eminent Persons on the Post-2015 Development Agenda. Paris, France and New York, USA: Sustainable Development Solutions Network. Available at http://unsdsn.org/resources

3. Inequality. (2013, March 13). Addressing Inequalities: Synthesis Report of Global Public Consultation. Co-led by UNICEF and UN Women with support from the Governments of Denmark and Ghana. Available at http://www.worldwewant2015.org/inequalities.

4. Melamed, C., and Samman, E. (2013, April). Equity, inequality and human development in a post-2015 framework. London, UK: Overseas Development Institute. Available at http://www.odi.org.uk/publications/7415-equityinequality-human-development-post-2015-framework

5. World Bank. (2012). World Development Report: Gender Equality and Development. Available at http://go.worldbank.org/6R2KGVEXP0

6. UN Secretary General. (2010). Women and peace and security. Security Council Report S/2010/173. New York, NY: United Nations. Available online at http://www.un.org/docs/sc/sgrep10.htm

7. UN Women (2013).A Transformative Stand-Alone Goal On Achieving Gender Equality, Women's Rights And Women's Empowerment: Imperatives And Key Components. New York, NY: United Nations. Available online at: http://www.unwomen.org/~/link.aspx?_id=981A49DCB34B44F1A84238A1E 02B6440and_z=z

8. Dijkstra & Hanmer (2000), Measuring socio-economic gender inequality: Toward an alternative to the UNDP gender-related development index, Feminist Economics, 6(2), pp 41-75

9. Tisdell, Roy & Ghose (2001), A critical note on UNDP's gender inequality indices, Journal of Contemporary Asia, 31(3), 385-399

10. Rao, E. Krishna (2006), "Role of Women in Agriculture: A Micro Level Study." Journal of Global Economy, Vol 2

11. Rao, E. Krishna (2006), "Role of Women in Agriculture: A Micro Level Study." Journal of Global Economy, Vol 2

12. Wichterich, Christa (2012) "The Other Financial Crisis: Growth and crash of the microfinance sector in India." Development 55.3: 406-412.

13. Unterhalther, E. (2006). Measuring Gender Inequality in South Asia. London: The United Nations Children's Fund (UNICEF).